Words for the Wedding

Words for the Wedding

Creative Ideas for Choosing and Using

Hundreds of Quotations to Personalize Your

Vows, Toasts, Invitations & More

WENDY PARIS and ANDREW CHESLER

A Perigee Book

A Perigee Book
Published by the Berkley Publishing Group
A division of Penguin Putnam Inc.
375 Hudson Street
New York, New York 10014

First edition: January 2001

Published simultaneously in Canada.

The Penguin Putnam Inc. World Wide Web site address is
http://www.penguinputnam.com

Library of Congress Cataloging-in-Publication Data

Paris, Wendy.
Words for the wedding : creative ideas for choosing and using hundreds of quotations
to personalize your vows, toasts, invitations, and more / Wendy Paris and Andrew Chesler.
p.   cm.
ISBN 0-399-52652-8
1. Wedding service.   2. Wedding etiquette.   3. Marriage—Quotations, maxims, etc.
4. Love—Quotations, maxims, etc.   5. Weddings—Quotations, maxims, etc.
I. Chesler, Andrew.   II. Title.

HQ745 .P36 2001
395.2'2—dc21
00-062374

Printed in the United States of America

10 9 8 7 6 5 4 3 2 1

To Amanda   To Thea

Contents

PART ONE

What to Say

READINGS, POETRY, PROSE AND QUOTES RELATING TO
WEDDINGS, MARRIAGE AND THE LOVE THEREIN

PART TWO

How to Say It

HOW TO USE READINGS, POETRY, PROSE AND QUOTES
TO CUSTOMIZE YOUR WEDDING

Acknowledgments

This book could not have come about without Thea Klapwald, who provided the idea, the initial research and the inspiration—and Amanda Robb, who helped with everything from writing the book proposal to reading the final draft. Or "drafts." Thanks to you both for your assistance and your continual, indefatigable support.

We'd like to thank our agent at New England Publishing Associates, Ed Knappman, for his professionalism, guidance and effort to find this book a home. Much thanks goes to our editor at Perigee, Shelia Curry Oakes, whose own pending nuptials made her the perfect person to work on this book. She never tired of the content and continually came up with the kinds of apt observations and suggestions only someone in the throes of the process could make.

Thanks go to George Prochnik for tracking down some of the most moving poems in this book and for providing invaluable writing inspiration. Thanks to Giles Lyon for sitting through endless romantic movies in search of quotes and for providing invaluable writing inspiration. Thanks to Anne Clarrissimeaux and David Ninh for last-minute research assistance, and to Dr. Carrie Anna Criado for helping find them. Thanks to both Ruth Kleinman and Pearl Solomon for their editorial assistance and good humor. And thanks to the librarians of, and contributors to, the New York Public Library.

Introduction

I want to go everywhere with you.
I want to go to Italy and Israel and down the street.
I want to lie on a raft under the sun in the South Pacific with you and
*   float and float and float.*
I want to go to the tallest building on the highest mountain in the biggest
*   city. And I want to go up on the roof with you and look around.*
I want us to pool our talents and pool our resources and create together,
*   that which we have not been able to create independently, alone.*
And I want you in smaller ways, too, right here, with me, holding my
*   hand and kissing me.*

That's what I'd want to say to the man I'd choose to marry. But there are many ways to express your feelings and make your wedding speak for the two of you—about a thousand of them right in this book.

Your wedding is unique because your relationship is unique. It's personal and specific. Don't let anyone tell you that they've been there before, they know the drill. They don't know. Only you do. Maybe your relationship started out as a friendship, something like *When Harry Met Sally.* Maybe your love swept over you instantly, knocking you flat on your back with the force of a tsunami and making you feel that unless you marry *this* person, and quickly, you will be washed away with the sand, or left to crawl uselessly to your end. Maybe you lived together for six years first, just to make sure it was the right thing . . .

Falling in love is better than anything else—it's better than sex, better than winning the lottery, better than a chocolate soufflé. Being free to bind yourself to the person you love is a kind of unbelievable good fortune not to be taken lightly or passed off as an obvious thing. It didn't have to happen. And it can fill your life, can lift you up in a way that nothing else can. There are so many of us, and it's always shocking and heartening and amazing to see one individual feel so strongly about another, as if this *one* person could really be that different from all the other six billion people on the planet. We are that different. And it's amazing.

Just as you didn't fall for any random person—but *this* person—don't settle for any old words to say your vows and seal your union. Find the right words. Use the quotes in this book, and the writing guidance in the second half, to help. Yes, they're just words. But expressing your feelings makes them stronger. Giving voice to your innermost emotions helps fortify their truth, solidify them as facts, make them stand up as beacons. Don't be afraid to say exactly what you mean.

Let your wedding be the seed of a continual flowering of expression. Challenge yourself, continually, to express just how much you love this person, and in what way, specifically. Talk about how much more inspired or intrigued or enlivened you are today than yesterday. And keep it up. Next year. And the next.

This book is called *Words for the Wedding.* But they're really words for the marriage. Use them wisely. Refer to them again and again. If you continually express how your love is evolving, you'll go a long way to ensuring that it will continue to do so.

—Wendy Paris

Words for the Wedding

Part 1

What To Say

Chapter 1

To Have and To Hold

Comfort

Now you will feel no rain,
For each of you will be shelter for the other.

Now you will feel no cold,
For each of you will be warmth to the other.

Now you will feel no loneliness.

Now you are two persons.
But, there is only one life before you.

Go now to your dwelling to enter
Into the days of your life together.

And may your days be good,
And long upon the earth.

—NATIVE AMERICAN MARRIAGE CEREMONY

Oh, the comfort, the inexpressible comfort of feeling safe with a person, having neither to weigh thoughts nor measure words, but pouring them all right out, just as they are, chaff and grain together; certain that a faithful hand will take and sift them, keep what is worth keeping, and then with the breath of kindness blow the rest away.

–DINAH MARIA MULOCK CRAIK, 19th-century poet and novelist

We seek the comfort of another. Someone to share and share the life we choose. Someone to help us through the never ending attempt to understand ourselves. And in the end, someone to comfort us along the way.

–MARLIN FINCH LUPUS

Now some people thinks it's jolly for to lead a single life,
But I believe in marriage and the comforts of a wife.
In fact you might have quarrels, just an odd one now and then,
It's worth your while a-falling out to make it up again.

–TRADITIONAL ENGLISH FOLK SONG

Wedlock is the deep, deep peace of the double bed after the hurly-burly of the chaise lounge.

–MRS. PATRICK CAMPBELL, early 20th-century English actress. The Irish-born British writer George Bernard Shaw wrote the character Eliza Doolittle in *Pygmalion* especially for her.

There is no more lovely, friendly and charming relationship, communion or company than a good marriage.

–MARTIN LUTHER, German 16th-century religious leader, founder of Protestantism

It's the strangest thing but I feel really safe with you. You know, like in old movies when people never left each other. I mean, they stayed together forever.

–HARRIET MICHAELS (ACTRESS NANCY TRAVIS) to Charlie Mackenzie
(ACTOR MIKE MYERS) in the movie *So I Married an Axe Murderer*

Come, let's be a comfortable couple and take care of each other! How glad we shall be, that we have somebody we are fond of always, to talk to and sit with. Let's be a comfortable couple. Now do, my dear!

–CHARLES DICKENS, 19th-century English novelist

Make the calculation—add up the items—and tell me if you don't think it a pity that you and I should live alone for thirty-two years, when we might as well be happy and comfortable together?

–AMELIA B. EDWARDS, 19th-century author, from *Hand and Glove*

There is no such cozy combination as man and wife.

–MENANDER, ancient Greek dramatist

A man reserves his greatest and deepest love not for the woman in whose company he finds himself electrified and enkindled but for that one in whose company he may feel tenderly drowsy.

–GEORGE JEAN NATHAN, American editor and drama critic

For indeed I never love you so well as when I think of sitting with you to dinner on a broiled scragg-end of mutton and hot potatoes. You then please my fancy more than when I think of you in . . . , no, you would never forgive me if I were to finish the sentence."

–WILLIAM HAZLITT, late 18th-/19th-century English essayist, to Sarah Stoddard, who he married, but divorced seven years later

Lay your sleeping head, my love,
Human on my faithless arm;
... in my arms till break of day
Let the living creature lie,
Mortal, guilty, but to me,
The entirely beautiful.

Soul and body have no bounds:
To Lovers as they lie upon
Her tolerant enchanted slope
In their ordinary swoon,
Grave the vision Venus sends
Of supernatural sympathy,
Universal love and hope ...

> –W. H. AUDEN, 20th-century English-born American poet from "Lay
> Your Sleeping Head"

We're too old to be single. Why shouldn't we both be married instead of sitting through the long winter evenings by our solitary firesides? Why shouldn't we make one fireside of it?

> –CHARLES DICKENS, 19th-century English novelist

Commitment

I am, as ever, in bewildered awe of anyone who makes this kind of commitment . . . I know I couldn't do it and I think it's wonderful they can.

> –CHARLES (ACTOR HUGH GRANT) giving the best man's toast in the movie
> *Four Weddings and a Funeral*

In a time when nothing is more certain than change, the commitment of two people to one another has become difficult and

rare. Yet, by its scarcity, the beauty and value of this exchange
have only been enhanced.

—ROBERT SEXTON, 20th-century poet and artist, from "The Vow"

When you call another woman
I will issue forth on your tongue,
Even as a taste of salt
Deep in the roots of your throat.
In hating, or singing, in yearning
It is me alone you summon . . .

—GABRIELA MISTRAL, 19th-/20th-century Chilean poet, from "God Wills It."

We cannot join ourselves to one another without giving our
word. And this must be an unconditional giving, for in joining
ourselves to one another we join ourselves to the unknown. We
can join one another only by joining the unknown. We must not
be misled by the procedures of experimental thought: in life, in
the world, we are never given two known results to choose between, but only one result: that we choose without knowing
what it is . . .

—WENDELL BERRY, contemporary poet and essayist, from *The Country of
Marriage*

A marriage between mature people is not an escape but a commitment shared by two people that becomes part of their commitment to themselves and society.

—BETTY FRIEDAN, 20th-century American feminist and writer

Conviction / Devotion

I haven't been so sure about anything since I got baptized.

> –DENISE MATTHEWS, the singer formerly known as Vanity, commenting
> on her marriage to football pro Anthony Smith

I knew it the minute I set eyes on you, you were the gal for me.
I'll go get cleaned up a bit and root out a preacher.

> –ADAM (ACTOR HOWARD KEEL) to Millie (ACTRESS JANE POWELL) in the
> movie *Seven Brides for Seven Brothers*

Go seek her out all courteously,
    And say I come,
Wind of spices whose song is ever
    Epithalamium.
O, hurry over the dark lands
    And run upon the sea
For seas and land shall not divide us
    My love and me.

Now, wind, of your good courtesy
    I pray you go,
And come into her little garden
    And sing at her window;
Singing: The bridal wind is blowing
    For Love is at his noon;
And soon will your true love be with you,
    Soon, O soon.

> –JAMES JOYCE, 20th-century Irish writer, poem XIII from *Chamber Music*

Go little ring to that same sweet
That hath my heart in her domain . . .

—GEOFFREY CHAUCER, 14th-century British author of *The Canterbury Tales*

If a man really loves a woman, of course he wouldn't marry her
for the world if he were not quite sure that he was the best person she could by any possibility marry.

—OLIVER WENDELL HOLMES, 19th-century American writer

I think we all know that when you fall in love, the emptiness
kind of drifts away . . . because you find something to live for.
Each other. And the way I see you two looking into each other's
eyes all day long, I can tell that you're going to live for each other
for the rest of your lives.

—ROBBIE, (ACTOR ADAM SANDLER), in the movie *The Wedding Singer*

When you realize you want to spend the rest of your life with
somebody, you want the rest of your life to start as soon as
possible.

—HARRY (ACTOR BILLY CRYSTAL) to Sally (ACTRESS MEG RYAN), in the movie
When Harry Met Sally

And Jacob served seven years for Rachel; and they seemed unto
him but a few days, for the love he had to her.

—GENESIS 29:20, *The Holy Bible,* King James version

My boat glides swiftly
beneath the wide cloud-ridden sky,
and as I look into the river

I can see the clouds drift by the moon;
my boat seems floating
on the sky.

And thus I dream
my beloved is mirrored
on my heart.

      –Tu Fu, 8th-century Chinese poet, from "On the River Tchou"

. . . Us. You, my bride, your voice speaks
Over the water to me.
Your hands, your solemn arms,
Cross the water and hold me.
Your body is beautiful.
It speaks across the water.
Bride, sweeter than honey, glad
Of heart, our hearts beat across
The bridge of our arms. Our speech
Is speech of the joy in the night
Of gladness. Our words live.
Our words are children dancing
Forth from us like stars on water.
My bride, my well beloved,
Sweeter than honey, than ripe fruit
Solemn, grave, a flying bird,
Hold me. Be quiet and kind.
I love you. Be good to me.
I am strong for you. I uphold
You. The dawn of ten thousand
Dawns is a fire in the sky.

The water flows in the earth.
The children laugh in the air.

> —KENNETH REXROTH, 20th-century American poet, from "The Old Song
> and Dance"

I will make you brooches and toys for your delight,
Of bird-song at morning and star-shine at night.
I will make you a palace fit for you and me,
Of green days in forests and blue days at sea.

> —ROBERT LOUIS STEVENSON, 19th-century Scottish novelist

If I could write the beauty of her eyes, I was born to look in
them and know myself.

> —WILL SHAKESPEARE (ACTOR JOSEPH FIENNES) to Lady Violet (ACTRESS
> GWYNETH PALTROW), in the movie *Shakespeare in Love*

To love someone is to see
a miracle invisible to others

> —FRANÇOIS MAURIAC, 19th-/20th-century French writer

I have spread my dreams under your feet;
Tread softly because you tread on my dreams.

> —WILLIAM BUTLER YEATS, 19th-/20th-century Irish poet and dramatist,
> from, "He Wishes for the Cloths of Heaven"

As the ant brought to Solomon the King
The thigh of a grass-hopper as an offering,
So do I bring my soul, beloved, to thee.

I have placed my head and my heart
On the sill of the door of my love.
Step gently, child!

   —LOVE SONG of the nomadic group of Turkish people known as the
   Turkoman

How much do I love thee?
Go ask the deep sea
How many rare gems
In its coral caves be,
Or ask the broad billows,
That ceaselessly roar
How many bright sands
So they kiss on the shore?

   —MARY ASHLEY TOWNSEND, 19th-century American essayist, poet and
   novelist

How do I love thee? Let me count the ways.
I love thee to the depth and breadth and height
My soul can reach, when feeling out of sight
For the ends of Being and ideal Grace.
I love thee to the level of every day's
Most quiet need, by sun and candlelight.
I love thee freely, as men strive for Right;
I love thee purely, as they turn from Praise.
I love thee with the passion put to use
In my old griefs, and with my childhood's faith,
I love thee with a love I seemed to lose
With my lost saints,—I love thee with the breath,
Smiles, tears, of all my life!—and, if God choose,
I shall but love thee better after death.

   —ELIZABETH BARRETT BROWNING, 19th-century British poet, known for her
   great love affair with her husband, Robert Browning, from "Sonnets
   from the Portuguese"

O my luve is like a red, red rose,
  That's newly sprung in June:
O my luve is like the melodie,
  That's sweetly play'd in tune.

As fair art thou, my bonnie lass,
  So deep in luve am I:
And I will luve thee still, my dear,
  Till a' the seas gang dry.

Till a' the seas gang dry, my dear,
  And the rocks melt wi' the sun;
And I will luve thee still my dear,
  While the sands o' life shall run.

And fare thee weel, my only luve!
  And fare thee weel a while!
And I will come again, my luve,
  Tho' it were ten thousand mile.

—ROBERT BURNS, 18th-century Scottish poet, from "A Red, Red Rose"

All paths lead to you
  Where e'er I stray,
You are the evening star
  At the end of day.

All paths lead to you
  Hill-top or low,
You are the white birch
  In the sun's glow.

All paths lead to you
    Where e'er I roam.
You are the lark-song

Calling me home!

        –Blanch Shoemaker Wagstaff, 19th-/20th-century writer

I see thee better—in the Dark—
I do not need a Light—
The Love of Thee—a Prism be—
Excelling Violet— . . .

What need of Day—
To Those whose Dark hath so—surpassing Sun—
It deem it be—Continually—
At the Meridian?

        –Emily Dickinson 19th-century American poet, from *The Complete Poems,*
          edited by Thomas H. Johnson

When our two souls stand up erect and strong,
Face to face, silent, drawing nigh and nigher
Until the lengthening wings break into fire
At either curved point,—what bitter wrong
Can the earth do us, that we should not long
Be here contented! Think. In mounting higher,
The angels would press on us and aspire
To drop some golden orb of perfect song
Into our deep, dear silence. Let us stay
Rather on earth, Beloved—where the unfit
Contrarious moods of men recoil away

And isolate pure spirits and permit
A place to stand and love in or a day . . .

> –ELIZABETH BARRETT BROWNING 19th-century poet, from "Sonnets from
> the Portuguese"

Distance—is not the Realm of Fox
Nor by Relay of Bird
Abated—Distance is
Until thyself, Beloved

> –EMILY DICKINSON, 19th-century American poet, from *The Complete
> Poems*, edited by Thomas H. Johnson

Some say cavalry and others claim
Infantry or a fleet of long oars
Is the supreme sight on the black earth.
I say it is

The one you love.

> –SAPPHO, Greek poet of the 7th-century, B.C.

You have become mine forever.
Yes, we have become partners.
I have become yours.
Hereafter, I cannot live without you.
Do not live without me.
Let us share the joys.
We are word and meaning, united.
You are thought and I am sound.

May the nights be honey-sweet for us.
May the mornings be honey-sweet for us.

May the plants be honey-sweet for us.
May the earth be honey-sweet for us.

—Hindu marriage poem

The voice of my beloved! behold, he cometh leaping upon the
    mountains, skipping upon the hills.
My beloved is like a rowe or a young hart: behold, he standeth
    behind our wall, he looketh forth at the windows, shewing
    himself through the lattice.

—Song of Solomon 2:8-9, *The Holy Bible,* King James version

Westley and I are joined by the bonds of love. And you cannot
track that, not with a thousand hounds. And you cannot break it,
not with a thousand swords.

—Buttercup (actress Robin Wright), in the movie *The Princess Bride*

You are my husband,
My feet shall run because of you.
My feet dance because of you.
My heart shall beat because of you.
My eyes see because of you.
My mind thinks because of you.
And I shall love because of you.

—Eskimo love song

He credited her with a number of virtues, of the existence of
which her conduct and conversation had given but limited indi-
cations. But, then, lovers have a proverbial power of balancing
inverted pyramids, going to sea in sieves, and successfully per-
forming kindred feats impossible to a faithless and unbelieving
generation.

—L. Malet

My fairest, my espous'd, my latest found,
Heaven's last best gift, my ever new delight!

> –JOHN MILTON, 17th-century English poet, from *Paradise Lost, Book V*

Listen to me, Mister. You're my knight in shining armor . . .
don't you forget it.

> –ETHEL THAYER (ACTRESS KATHARINE HEPBURN), to Norman Thayer (ACTOR
> HENRY FONDA), in the movie *On Golden Pond*

No man ever forgot the visitation of that power to his heart and
brain, which created all things anew; which was the dawn in
him of music, poetry and art; which made the face of nature ra-
diant with purple light, the morning and the night varied en-
chantments; . . . when he became all eye when one was present,
and all memory when one was gone.

> –RALPH WALDO EMERSON, 19th-century American poet and essayist

I got me flowers to strew Thy way;
I got me boughs off many a tree:
But Thou wast up by break of day,
And brought'st Thy sweets along with Thee.

The Sunne arising in the East,
Though He give light & th' East perfume;
If they should offer to contest
With Thy arising, they presume.

Can there be any day but this,
Though many sunnes to shine endeavour?
We count three hundred, but we misse:
There is but one, and that one ever.

> –GEORGE HERBERT, 17th-century English poet, from "Easter"

I almost wish we were butterflies and liv'd but three summer days—three such days with you I could fill with more delight than fifty common years could ever contain . . .

> –JOHN KEATS, 19th-century English poet, in a letter to Fanny Brawne, dated July 1, 1819

No angel she; she hath no budding wings;
    No mystic halo circles her bright hair;
But lo! the infinite grace of little things,
    Wrought for dear love's sake, makes her very fair.

> –JAMES BENJAMIN KENYON, 19th-century writer

. . . walk through life in dreams
out of love of the hand that leads us.

> –ANTONIO MACHADO, 19th-/20th-century Spanish poet, from "Rebirth," translated by Robert Bly

Though heaven's wheel be mired down, lovers' lives go forward.
Let other people be downcast, the lover is blissful and sprightly.
Invite a lover into each dark corner. The lover is bright as a
    hundred thousand candles!
Even if a lover seems to be alone, the secret Beloved is nearby.

> –JALĀL AL-DĪN RŪMĪ, 13th-century Persian poet

But if you tame me, then we shall need each other. To me, you will be unique in all the world. To you, I shall be unique in all the world.

> –ANTOINE DE SAINT-EXUPÉRY, 20th-century French writer, from the children's story *The Little Prince*

This is a charm I set for love; a woman's charm of love and desire;
A charm of God that none can break: You for me and I for thee
    and for none else;
Your face to mine and your head turned away from all others.

    –IRISH SAYING

I am a crystal goblet in my Love's hand.
Look into my eyes if you don't believe me.

    –JALĀL AL-DĪN RŪMĪ, 13th-century Persian poet

I wonder by my troth, what thou, and I
Did, till lov'd? were we not wean'd till then
But suck'd on countrey pleasures, childishly?
Or snorted we in the seaven sleeper den?
T'was so; But this, all pleasures fancies bee.
If ever any beauty I did see,
Which I desir'd, and got, t'was but a dreame of thee.

And now good morrow to our waking soules,
Which watch not one another out of feare;
For love, all love of other sights controules,
And make one little roome, an every where.
Let sea-discoverers to new world have gone,
Let Maps to other, worlds on worlds have showne,
Let us possesse one world, each hath one, and is one.

My face in thine eye, thine in mine apears,
And true plaine hearts doe in the faces rest,
Where can we finde two better hemispheares
Without sharpe North, without declining West?
Why ever dyes, was not mixt equally;

If our two loves be one, or thou and I
Love so alike, that none doe slacken, none can die.

> –JOHN DONNE, 16th-/17th-century English poet and clergyman, from
> "The Good Morrow"

Courtship

If you don't marry him, you haven't caught him, he's caught you.

> –SHOTZIE (ACTRESS LAUREN BACALL), explaining to her coconspirators the
> necessity of setting a marriage "bear trap" for suitors, in the movie *How
> to Marry a Millionaire*

It was so much fun we proposed to each other all day long.

> –ACTRESS MELISSA ERRICO, commenting on being proposed to by tennis
> star Patrick McEnroe

More than kisses, letters mingle souls.

> –JOHN DONNE, 16th-/17th-century English poet and clergyman

Dearest,—I wish I had the gift of making rhymes, for methinks there is poetry in my head and heart since I have been in love with you. You are a Poem. Of what sort, then? Epic? Mercy on me, no! A sonnet? No; for that is too labored and artificial. You are a sort of sweet, simple, gay, pathetic ballad, which Nature is singing, sometimes with tears, sometimes with smiles and sometimes with intermingled smiles and tears.

> –NATHANIEL HAWTHORNE, 19th-century American writer, to Sophia
> Peabody

I like not only to be loved, but also to be told that I am loved. I am not sure that you are of the same kind. But the realm of silence is large enough beyond the grave. This is the world of light and speech, and I shall take leave to tell you that you are very dear.

–GEORGE ELIOT, 19th-century English novelist

The reason why lovers are never weary of one another is this— they are always talking of themselves.

–FRANÇOIS DE LA ROCHEFOUCAULD, 17th-century French writer, from *Maxims and Reflections*

A beauty is a woman you notice; A charmer is one who notices you.

–ADLAI STEVENSON, 20th-century American politician

The plainest man that can convince a woman that he is really in love with her has done more to make her in love with him than the handsomest man, if he can produce no such conviction. For the love of woman is a shoot, not a seed, and flourishes most vigorously only when ingrafted on that love which is rooted in the breast of another.

–CHARLES CALEB COLTON, 18th-/19th-century writer and poet, from *Lacon*

We attract hearts by the qualities we display: we retain them by the qualities we possess.

–JEAN SUARD, 18th-/19th-century French writer

Courtship to marriage is but as the music in the playhouse till the curtain's drawn.

–WILLIAM CONGREVE, 17th- and 18th-century British dramatist

Things are a little different now. First you have to be friends. You have to like each other. Then you neck, this could go on for years. Then you have tests. Then you get to do it with a condom. The good news is you split the check.

> –JAY (ACTOR ROB REINER), in the movie *Sleepless in Seattle*

Once it was see somebody, get excited, get married. Now it's read a lot of books, fence with a lot of four-syllable words, psychoanalyze each other until you can't tell the difference between a petting party and a civil service exam.

> –STELLA (ACTRESS THELMA RITTER), from the movie *Rear Window*

I am very certain that if we were married together, it would not be long before we should both be very miserable. My wife must have a character directly opposite to my dear Zelide, except in affection, in honesty, and in good humour . . .

Defend yourself . . . Tell me that you will make a very good wife.

> –JAMES BOSWELL, Scottish biographer who wrote *Life of Johnson,* from a letter to the daughter of a prominent Dutch family. He was turned down.

Whatever woman may cast her lot with mine, should any ever do so, it is my intention to do all in my power to make her happy and contented; and there is nothing I can imagine that would make me more unhappy than to fail in the effort.

> –ABRAHAM LINCOLN, 16th U.S. president, to Mary Owens in a letter from Springfield, Illinois, dated 1837. Owens rejected him.

"I am very happy," said Popinot. "If you would lighten all my fears—in a year I shall be so prosperous that your father cannot object when I speak to him of our marriage. From henceforth I will sleep only five hours a night."

"Do not injure yourself," said Cesarine, with an inexpressible accent, and a look in which Popinot was suffered to read her thoughts.

—Honoré de Balzac, 19th-century French novelist who portrayed the foibles and fashions of French society, from *Cesar Birotteau*

I can boast not wealth nor birth
Think you these alone have worth
Surely health, a heart that's true
A hand that can protect you too,
Are gems and these I proffer you.

—From a Victorian card

Come here to me, we'll put an end to all the gossip, exchange rings, pay our visits, and then we'll be betrothed . . .

I even love all the perfectly mad things that you do; when you lie, you lie as only a poet, as only I can lie; I love you because your mouth is so beautiful and your little teeth are so pearly white; when you're angry I love you because your deep eyes spit fire; I love you because you're so horribly clever and greedy, because you write your disagreegable business letters for my sake.

—August Strindberg, 19th-/20th-century Swedish dramatist and novelist, to Frieda Uhl, who became his second wife

The great and profound request which I take the liberty to address to you herewith, Fräulein Josefine, is this: Would Fräulein Josefine kindly give her frank final and decisive answer, in writing for my future calm, to the question: May I hope and ask your dear parents for your hand? . . . Once more I beg you: Write frankly and sincerely: either that I may propose, or a complete and permanent refusal (please no compromise to console or evade the point, for it is high time for me), and your feelings will probably not change because Fräulein is reasonable. Fräulein

Josefine may say the whole truth without fear because in any case it will give me peace of mind.

Expecting a decisive answer as soon as possible, I kiss your hand.

> —ANTON BRUCKNER, 19th-century Austrian composer, to Josefine Lang, who turned him down. He never married.

May we be permitted to hope that you will receive graciously the feelings which impel us to take this step? May we harbor the flattering hope that you will agree to this marriage not only because of filial obedience and duty?

If your imperial Highness has but the slightest affection for us we will cultivate this feeling with the greatest pains, and make it our supreme task ever to seek your happiness in every respect. In this way we fondly hope to win your complete affection some day. That is our most fervent wish, and we beg your Imperial Highness to be favorably inclined to us.

> —EMPEROR NAPOLEON I to the Archduchess Maria Louise of Austria, in a letter from Rambouillet dated February 23, 1810. They married later that year.

Thank God it is not a dream; Jane loves me! She loves me! And I swear by the Immortal Powers that she shall yet be mine, as I am hers, through life and death and all the dark vicissitudes that wait us here and hereafter.

> —THOMAS CARLYLE, 19th-century Scottish historian and essayist, to Jane Welsh in 1823. They married.

Summon all the courage of your heart in order not to be shocked by the question I shall put to you: Will you marry me? . . .

Do you not also believe that, united, we could become freer and better than separate—excelsior? Will you risk going with me—as with one who struggles valiantly for liberation and progress on all the paths of life and thought?

–Friedrich Nietzsche, 19th-century German philosopher, to Mathilde Trampedach in a letter from Geneva, dated 1876. She turned him down.

Don't you agree that if a man says he loves a girl he ought to marry her?

–Tracey Lord (actress Katharine Hepburn), in the movie *Philadelphia Story*

Marry Joan, cry I still, but wilt thou marry me, Joan? I know thou doest love Will the Taylor, who, it is true, is a very quiet man and foots it most fetuously; but I can tell thee, Joan, I think I shall be a better man than he very shortly, for I am learning of a fiddler to play on the kit, so that if you will not yield the sooner, I will ravish thee ere long with my music . . . Law ye what a happy day that would be, to see thee with thy best clothes on, at Church, and the Parson saying, I, Hodge, take thee Joan, and by the Mass I would take thee and hug thee and buss thee, and then away to the Alehouse . . .

–Samuel Richardson, 18th-century English writer, from *Familiar Letters on Important Occasions*

My beloved spake, and said unto me, Rise up, my love, my fair one, and come away.

For, lo, the winter is past, the rain is over and gone;

The flowers appear on the earth; the time of the singing of birds is come, and the voice of the turtle is heard in our land;

The fig tree putteth forth her green figs, and the vines with the tender grape give a good smell. Arise, my love, my fair one, and come away.

–Song of Solomon 2:10-13, *The Holy Bible,* King James version

I begin this letter by indicating its contents; it is to ask you for the supreme thing that you can give away in this world: the hand of your daughter. I know I seem audacious if, known to you only recently and from sparse meetings, I ask you for the highest proof of trust that you can give to a man. I also know that, apart from all handicaps of space and time which might make it difficult for you to form an opinion of me, I shall by myself never be able to give you such security for the future as would warrant the handing over of such a precious pledge, unless you complete by faith in God what faith in man cannot do.

–PRINCE OTTO VON BISMARCK, later chancellor of the German Reich, to
the father of his future wife, Johanna von Puttkamer, in 1846

When [she] surrendered, it was with a shy, reluctant grace. Hers was not a passionate nature, but a loving one; feeling with her was not a single, simple emotion, but a complicated one of many impulses—of self-diffidences, of deep, strange aspirations that she herself could scarcely understand.

–ANNE THACKERAY RITCHIE, 19th-century novelist, from *Old Kensington*

"Come here, Véronique," said Gordon Romilly, holding out his arms to receive her, "come here, and tell me, if you'll be my little wife?"

"Votre femme," exclaimed the girl, without moving from her position, *"Monsieur! C'est impossible, je ne peux pas le croire."*

"Say that it shall be so, Véronique, and I'll soon make you believe it! But, perhaps, you would rather not?"

"Monsieur!" In a tone of remonstrance.

"Well, come down here, then, and tell me what you wish."

She advanced a few steps timidly toward him, and he put out his hand and pulled her down the remainder of the flight, until she rested in the circle of his embrace.

"Will you marry me, Véronique?" Kissing her.

"Mais oui, Monsieur."

"Will you be my wife?" Kissing her again.

"Mais oui, Monsieur."

"Will you ever call me, 'Monsieur' again?"

"Mais oui, Monsieur," replied Véronique, not knowing what she said.

–FLORENCE MARRYATT, 19th-century novelist, from *Véronique*

Cory: But you never had a first date!

Lloyd: Yes, I did. I sat across from her at the mall. We ate to-gether. We ate. That's eating, sharing an important physical event.

–COREY FLOOD (ACTRESS LILI TAYLOR) to Lloyd Dobler (ACTOR JOHN CUSACK), in the movie *Say Anything*

All things do go a-courting,
In earth, or sea, or air,
God hath made nothing single
But thee in His world so fair.

–EMILY DICKINSON, 19th-century American writer

Think not because you now are wed
That all your courtship's at an end.

–ANTONIO HURTADO DE MENDOZA, 16th-/17th-century Spanish poet

The Oriole weds his mottled mate,
The Lily weds the bee;
Heaven's marriage ring is round the earth,
Let me bind thee?

–FROM A VICTORIAN CARD

I cannot sleep but with a great deal of disturbance, I have not the same advantage of air as other men, I do not so much breathe as sigh. This is the condition I have been in ever since I saw you last, and now, Madam, that I have made known my torments to you. Give me leave to tell you that there is nothing in this world can give me anything of ease but one line from your Ladyship, for which I as earnestly beg as I would for a morsel of bread if I were ready to starve . . . I beg that you would be pleased sometime that I am, Madam, your Ladyship's most humble and dutiful servant.

–JOHN RUSSELL, 19th-century English statesman, to Lady Frances Rich, daughter of Oliver Cromwell. She agreed to marry him.

You might be happy without me—you could never be unhappy through me. You might give yourself to another, but none could love you more purely or tenderly than I. To no one could your happiness be more sacred than it was and always will be to me. I dedicate my very existence and everything in me, everything, my dearest, to you, and if I strive to make myself more noble, it is only to make myself more worthy of you, to make you happier . . .

I consign all the joys of my life to you. I can think of my joys under no other form than your image.

–FRIEDRICH VON SCHILLER, 19th-/20th-century German dramatist and writer, to Charlotte von Lengefeldt. She agreed to marry him.

You are apprehensive of losing your liberty; but could you but think with how many domestic pleasures the sacrifice will be repaid, you would no longer think it very frightful.

–SIR WALTER SCOTT, 19th-century Scottish poet and novelist, to his future wife, Charlotte Carpenter

Oh, Bathsheba, promise—it is only a little promise—that if you marry again, you will marry me!

> –THOMAS HARDY, 19th-/20th-century English novelist and poet, from *Far from the Madding Crowd*

Johnny, it's for luck. I mean, a man proposes to a woman, he should kneel down.

> –LORETTA (CHER), in the movie *Moonstruck*

In times past (as I remember) you were minded that I should marry you . . . and puts me upon enquiring whether you will be willing that I should Marry you now, by becoming your Husband; Aged, and feeble, and exhausted as I am, your favorable Answer to this Enquiry, in a few Lines, the Candor of it will much oblige, Madam, your humble Servt.

> –SAMUEL SEWALL, 17th-/18th-century colonial American jurist, to the Widow Gibbs, who agreed to become his third wife

Come live with me and be my love,
And we will some new pleasures prove,
Of golden sands and crystal brooks,
With silken lines and silver hooks

> –JOHN DONNE, 16th-/17th-century English poet and clergyman, from "The Bait"

Come live with me and be my love,
And we will all the pleasures prove
That valleys, groves, hills, and fields,
Woods, or steepy mountains yields.
And we will sit upon the rocks,

Seeing the shepherds feed their flocks,
By shallow rivers to whose falls
Melodious birds sing madrigals.

And I will make thee beds of roses
And a thousand fragrant posies,
A cap of flowers, and a kirtle
Embroidered all with leaves of myrtle;

A gown made of the finest wool
Which from our pretty lambs we pull;
Fair lined slippers for the cold,
With buckles of the purest gold;

A belt of straw and ivy buds,
With coral clasps and amber studs:
And if these pleasures may thee move,
Come live with me, and be my love.

The shepherds' swains all dance and sing
For thy delight each May morning:
If these delights thy mind may move,
Then live with me and be my love.

> –CHRISTOPHER MARLOWE, 16th-century English dramatist, from "The Passionate Shepherd to His Love"

Set me as a seal upon thine heart, as a seal upon thine arm: for love is strong as death; jealousy is cruel as the grave; the coals thereof are coals of fire, which hath a most vehement flame.

Many waters cannot quench love, neither can the floods drown it: if a man would give all the substance of his house for love, it would utterly be contemned.

> –SONG OF SOLOMON 8:6-7, *The Holy Bible,* King James version

In a word, you must give me either a fan, a mask, or a glove you have worn, or I cannot live; otherwise you must expect I'll kiss your hand, or, when I next sit by you, steal your handkerchief. You yourself are too great a bounty to be received at once; therefore I must be prepared by degree, lest the might gift distract me with joy.

> –RICHARD STEELE, English essayist, playwright, and statesman, in 1707, to Mary Scurlock. They later married.

Talking of widows—pray, Eliza, if ever you are such, do not think of giving yourself to some wealthy Nabob—because I design to marry you myself. My wife cannot live long—she has sold all the provinces in France already—I know not the woman I should like so well for her substitute as yourself.

> –LAURENCE STERNE, 18th-century English novelist, to Eliza Draper, a married woman who declined his advances

Juliet: Good-night, good-night, as sweet repose and rest
           Come to thy heart as that within my breast!

Romeo: O! wilt though leave me so unsatisfied?

Juliet: What satisfaction canst thou have tonight?

Romeo: The exchange of thy love's faithful vow for mine.

Juliet: I gave thee mine before thou didst request it,
           And yet I would it were to give again.

Romeo: Wouldst thou withdraw it? for what purpose, love?

Juliet: But to be frank, and give it thee again.
           And yet I wish but for the thing I have.
           My bounty is as boundless as the sea,

My love as deep; the more I give to thee,
The more I have, both are infinite.

–WILLIAM SHAKESPEARE, 16th-/17th-century English poet and playwright,
from *Romeo and Juliet*

More than forty-eight hours have passed without my taking the smallest nourishment. Oh let me not live so. Death is certainly better than this—which if in forty-eight hours it has not occurred must follow; for by all that is holy, till I am married I will eat nothing, and if I am not married the promise will die with me. I am resolute. Nothing shall alter my resolution.

–AUGUSTUS FREDERICK, Duke of Sussex, in a letter to Lady Augusta Murray, dated 1820. She agreed to marry him.

I would have laughed myself sick a month ago if I had been told that I would suffer, suffer joyfully, as I have been doing for this past month. Tell me, with all the candor that is yours: Will you be my wife? If you can say *yes, boldly,* with all your heart, then *say it,* but if you have the faintest shadow of doubt, say *no.* For heaven's sake, think it over carefully. I am terrified to think of a *no,* but I am prepared for it and will be strong enough to bear it. But it will be terrible if I am not loved by my wife as much as I love you!

–LEO TOLSTOY, 19th-century Russian novelist, to his future wife, Sonya-Bers, in 1862

I wish I were a young lord and you were unmarried. I should make you the best husband in the world . . .

–JONATHAN SWIFT, 17th-/18th-century English author and satirist, in 1727

Tell me what you intend to do for me. I will take infinite pains to deserve your love and friendship, and will always strive to keep you from regretting your decision to marry me. There is just one more thing I must mention: I have a daughter ten years of age, whom I idolize.

> –FIELD MARSHAL GEBHARD LEBERCHT VON BLÜCHER, 18th-/19th-century Prussian general, to Frau von S. in 1795. Discretion prevented him from using her full name. He withdrew his proposal "because of too unequal fortunes."

Dear Charles,
On the basis of affection, admiration and common interests I should find marrying you a delightful pact for mutual benefit. Should it, as a contract, prove otherwise, I assure you I would be entirely tractable and undemanding; if a mistake emotionally speaking, I assure you—"that I can go like snow and leave no trace behind."

> –ALICE

> –Letter from the 1920s or '30s cited in *Will You Marry Me?* by Helene Scheu-Riesz

Who shall have my fair lady!
Who but I, who but I, who but I?
Under the green leaves!
The fairest man
That best love can,
Under the green leaves!

> –ANONYMOUS

—Consent, consent, consent to be
—My many-branched, small and dearest tree.

> –DELMORE SCHWARTZ, 20th-century American poet, from "Will You Perhaps Consent to Be"

There is only one situation I can think of in which men and women make an effort to read better than they usually do. When they are in love and reading a love letter, they read for all they are worth. They read every word three ways; they read between the lines and in the margins . . . They may even take the punctuation into account. Then, if never before or after, they read.

–MORTIMER ADLER, 20th-century century American dramatist and philosopher

I will teach her to know that the man who loves her can seek no other wife;—that no other mode of living is possible to him . . . than one in which he and Marion Fay shall be joined together. I think I shall persuade her at last that such is the case. I think she will come to know that all her cold prudence and worldly would-be wisdom can be of no avail to separate those who love each other. I think that when she finds that her lover so loves her that he cannot live without her, she will abandon those fears as to his future fickleness, and trust herself to one of whose truth she will have assured herself.

–ANTHONY TROLLOPE, 19th-century English novelist, from *Marion Fay*

Marry, if you can feel love; marry, and be happy. Honor! Virtue! Yes, I have both; and I will not forfeit them. Yes, I will merit your esteem and my own—by actions, not words . . .

–MARIA EDGEWORTH, 19th-century novelist, from *The Absentee*

"If I speak clumsily, I will ask you to excuse me. I have only known you for three months , and that is but a little time. I should have laughed three months ago to think that such a love"—the word cost him great and evident effort, and it was plain that it was sacred to him; the listener knew it—"could have grown in a man's heart in such a time. But it has grown there, and my life is in your hands. I ask a great thing—I ask a thing of which I know I am unworthy—I ask you to share my life with me. It shall be my continual study to make you happy." There his very earnestness broke him down.

". . . Give me an answer now!" he murmured, with pleading eyes fastened on her face—"give me an answer now!" This was a phase of love-making on which Constance had not counted, and it was new to her. The man was kissing one hand, and had possessed himself of the other,—a prodigious and unheard-of situation. It was not unpleasant, though at first a little alarming. "Say Yes," said this audacious Gerard, murmuring with his breath upon her cheek, and both her hands in his.

And it was wonderful and strange—if Nature were ever wonderful and strange—to see how the stronger male nature triumphed; for caught in this unexpected snare, wooed for once like a woman, by a man who loved her, in place of being talked to by an automaton as though she were an elegant wax-work, she answered, "Yes;" and for one bewildered minute her head lay on Gerard's shoulder, and the first kiss that ever love had planted there was warm upon her lips.

–D. CHRISTIE MURRAY, 19th-century writer, from the novel *Val Strange*

"Don't call honest love foolishness . . . Sure, why would we have hearts in our bodies if we didn't love? Sure, our hearts would be of no use at all without we wor[sic] fond of one another . . . I must have your answer.

–SAMUEL LOVER, 19th-century Anglo-Irish writer, from his novel, *Rory O'More*

Miss Adorable

By the same Token that the Bearer hereof satt up with you last night I hereby order you to give him, as many Kisses, and as many Hours of your Company after 9 O'clock as he shall please to Demand and charge them to my Account: This Order, or Requisition call it which you will is in Consideration of a similar order Upon Aurelia for the like favour, and I presume I have good Right to draw upon you for the Kisses as I have given two or three Millions at least, when one has been received, and of Consequence the Account between us is immensely in favour of.

> Yours,
> John Adams

–JOHN ADAMS, 2nd U.S. president, to his future wife, Abigail Smith

Faith

O Lord Fire, First Created Being! Be thou the over-lord and give food and drink to this household. O Lord Fire, who reigns in richness and vitality over all the worlds, come take your proper seat in this home! Accept the offerings made here, protect the one who makes them, be our protector on this day, O you who see into the hearts of all created beings!

–HINDU WEDDING PRAYER

I will greatly rejoice in the LORD, my soul shall be joyful in my God; for he hath clothed me with the garments of salvation, he hath covered me with the robe of righteousness, as a bridegroom decketh himself with ornaments, and as a bride adorneth herself with her jewels.

For as the earth bringeth forth her bud, and as the garden causeth the things that are sown in it to spring forth; so the Lord GOD will cause righteousness and praise to spring forth before all nations.

–ISAIAH 61:10-11, *The Holy Bible,* King James version

To love another person is to help them love God.

–SÖREN KIERKEGAARD, 19th-century Danish philosopher

The love of God, unutterable and perfect,
flows into a pure soul the way that light
rushes into a transparent object.
The more love that it finds, the more it gives
itself, so that, as we grow clear and open,
the more complete the joy of living is.
And the more souls who resonate together,
the greater the intensity of their love,
for, mirror-like, each soul reflects the other.

–DANTE, 13th-/14th-century Italian poet, from "The Love of God"

That nothing may be between me and her, be thou between us, every moment. That we may be constantly together, draw us into separate loneliness with thyself. And when we meet breast to breast, my God, let it be on thine own. Amen. Amen.

–TEMPLE GAIRDNER, in a prayer before his marriage

And he answered and said unto them, Have ye not read, that he which made them at the beginning made them male and female,

And said, For this cause shall a man leave father and mother, and shall cleave to his wife: and they twain shall be one flesh?

Wherefore they are no more twain, but one flesh. What therefore God hath joined together, let not man put asunder.

–MATTHEW 19:4-6, *The Holy Bible,* King James version

Socrates: [Love] is a great spirit intermediate between the divine and the mortal.

–PLATO, ancient Greek philosopher, from the *Symposium*

That I may come near to her, draw me nearer to thee than to her; that I may know her, make me to know thee more than her; that I may love her with the perfect love of a perfectly whole heart, cause me to love thee more than her and most of all Amen. Amen.

–TEMPLE GAIRDNER, in a prayer before his marriage

Family

We called both moms but told each that she was the first one we called. It's such a secret that I can't remember which one we actually called first.

–ACTOR JOHN STAMOS, on proposing to supermodel Rebecca Romijn

You know what they say, "My son's my son until he gets him a wife but my daughter's my daughter all of her life."

–STANLEY BANKS (ACTOR SPENCER TRACY), in the movie *Father of the Bride* (1950)

Family love is this dynastic awareness of time, this shared belonging to a chain of generations . . . we collaborate together to
root each other in a dimension of time longer than our own lives.

–MICHAEL IGNATIEFF, contemporary Canadian-born writer, from *Lodged in
the Heart and Memory*

Fate

A good marriage is at least eighty percent good luck in finding
the right person at the right time. The rest is trust.

–NANETTE NEWMAN, British actress

It was a million tiny little things that, when you added them all
up, they meant we were supposed to be together . . . and I knew
it. I knew it the very first time I touched her. It was like coming
home . . . the only real home I'd ever known. I was just taking
her hand to help her out of a car. It was like . . . magic.

–SAM BALDWIN (ACTOR TOM HANKS), in the movie *Sleepless in Seattle*

Oh,
I am thinking
Oh,
I am thinking
I have found
My lover,
Oh,
I think it is so.

–CHIPPEWA SONG

"O love,
    where are you
    leading
    me now?"

> –Robert Creeley, contemporary American poet, from "Kore"

All those broken relationships. All those men. It must have hurt going through so many guys and never finding the right one. And all the while the man of your dreams was right in front of you.

> –Kimmy (actress Cameron Diaz) to Julia (actress Julie Roberts), in the movie *My Best Friend's Wedding*

. . . You are the only being whom I can love absolutely with my complete self, with all my flesh and mind and heart. You are my mate, my perfect partner, and I am yours . . . It is some kind of divine luck that we are together now. We must never, never part again. We are, here in this, necessary beings, like gods. As we look at each other, we verify, we know the perfection of our love, we recognize each other. Here is my life, here if need be is my death.

> –Iris Murdoch, 20th-century English novelist, from *The Book and the Brotherhood*

Nothing happens without a cause. The union of this man and woman has not come about accidentally but is the foreordained result of many past lives. This tie can therefore not be broken or dissolved.

> –Buddhist marriage homily

When you're attracted to someone it just means that your sub-conscious is attracted to their subconscious, subconsciously, so what we know as fate is that they're two neuroses knowing that they're a perfect match.

> –DENNIS REED (ACTOR DAVID HYDE PIERCE), in the movie *Sleepless in Seattle*

The moment I heard my first love story I began seeking you,
Not realizing the search was useless.
Lovers don't meet somewhere along the way.
They're in one another's souls from the beginning.

> –JALĀL AL-DĪN RŪMĪ, 13th-century Persian poet, adapted from the transla-
> tion by A. J. Arberry

People do belong to each other. Because that's the only chance anybody's got for real happiness.

> –PAUL VARJACK (ACTOR GEORGE PEPPARD) to Holly Golightly (ACTRESS
> AUDREY HEPBURN), in the movie *Breakfast at Tiffany's*

Oh, hasten not this loving act,
Rapture where self and not-self meet:
My life has been the awaiting you,
Your footfall was my own heart's beat.

> –PAUL VALÉRY, 19th-/20th-century French poet and philosopher

... the apparently uneventful and stark moment at which our future sets foot in us is so much closer to life than that other noisy and fortuitous point of time at which it happens to us as if from outside ... We have ... to realize that which we call des-tiny goes forth from within people, not from without into them.

> –RAINER MARIA RILKE, 19th-/20th-century German poet, from *Letters to a
> Young Poet,* translation by M. D. Herter Norton

Destiny is something we've invented because we can't stand the fact that everything that happens is accidental.

–ANNIE REED (ACTRESS MEG RYAN), in the movie *Sleepless in Seattle*

Diane: Nobody thinks it will work, do they?

Lloyd: No. You just described every great success story.

–DIANE COURT (ACTRESS IONE SKYE) and Lloyd Dobler (ACTOR JOHN CUSACK) in the movie *Say Anything*

Follow Your Heart, Not Your Head

The heart has its reasons of which reason knows nothing.

–BLAISE PASCAL, 17th-century French mathematician and philosopher, *Pensées,* translated by A. J. Krailsheimer

True, we love life, not because we are used to living, but because we are used to loving. There is always some madness in love, but there is also always some reason in madness.

–FRIEDRICH NIETZSCHE, 19th-century German philosopher, from *Thus Spake Zarathustra*

We should marry to please ourselves, not other people.

–ISAAC BICKERSTAFFE, 18th-century English dramatist

Jeff: There's an intelligent way to approach marriage.

Stella: Nothing has caused the human race so much trouble as intelligence.

–JEFF (ACTOR JAMES STEWART) and Stella (ACTRESS THELMA RITTER), in the movie *Rear Window*

"And now here is my secret, a very simple secret: it is only with the heart that one can see rightly; what is essential is invisible to the eye . . ."

—ANTOINE DE SAINT-EXUPERY, 20th-century French writer, from *The Little Prince,* translated by Katherine Woods

"The heart? Ask it. Nothing is surer."

—GEORGE MEREDITH, 19th-century novelist, from *Beauchamp's Career*

There is more of good nature than of good sense at the bottom of most marriages.

—HENRY DAVID THOREAU, 19th-century American writer

. . . anything may take place at any time, for love does not care for time or order . . .

—"ON KISSING" FROM *THE KAMA SUTRA OF VATSYAYANA,* the Hindu treatise on love

Happiness, Joy and Laughter

The highest happiness on earth is marriage.

—WILLIAM LYON PHELPS, 19th-/20th-century American educator, author and critic

There is not earthly happiness exceeding that of a reciprocal satisfaction in the conjugal state.

—W. GILES

Despite all the protestations of men to the contrary, married life makes them happy.

> —Jessie Bernard, contemporary author and sociologist

My marriage was much the most fortunate and joyous event which happened to me in my whole life.

> —Winston Churchill, Britain's Prime Minister (1940–45 and 1950–51)

Marriage is the most natural state of man, and the state in which you will find solid happiness.

> —Benjamin Franklin, 18th-century American patriot, diplomat, author, printer, scientist and inventor

A happy marriage is a long conversation that always seems too short.

> —André Maurois, 20th-century French writer

The intense happiness of our union is derived in a high degree from the perfect freedom with which we each follow and declare our own impressions.

> —George Eliot, 19th-century English novelist

Remember this . . . that very little is needed to make a happy life.

> —Marcus Aurelius, Roman emperor and philosopher

A happy marriage is a new beginning of life, a new starting point for happiness and usefulness.

> —A. P. Stanley

The supreme happiness of life is the conviction of being loved for yourself, or, more correctly being loved in spite of yourself.

–VICTOR HUGO, 19th-century French dramatist, novelist and poet

. . . Mutual love, the crown of all our bliss.

–JOHN MILTON, 17th-century English poet, *Paradise Lost, Book IV*

It takes patience to appreciate domestic bliss; volatile spirits prefer unhappiness.

–GEORGE SANTAYANA, 19th-/20th-century American philosopher

I am most
immoderately married:
The Lord God has taken
my heaviness away,
I have merged, like the bird,
with the bright air,
And my thought flies
to the place by the bo-tree.
Being, not doing,
is my first joy.

–THEODORE ROETHKE, 20th-century American poet, from *The Abyss*

One year of Joy, another of Comfort, and all the rest of content, make the married Life happy.

–THOMAS FULLER, 17th-century English author

Already the second day since our marriage, his love and gentle-ness is beyond everything, and to kiss that dear soft cheek, to press my lips to his, is heavenly bliss. I feel a purer more un-earthly feel than I ever did. Oh! was ever a woman so blessed as I am.

> —QUEEN VICTORIA OF GREAT BRITAIN, from an entry in her journal dated
> February, 1840

Married love is love woven into a pattern of living. It has in it the elements of understanding and of the passionate kindness of husband and wife toward each other. It is rich in the many-sided joys of life because each is more concerned with giving joy than with grasping it for himself. And joys are most truly experienced when they are most fully shared.

> —LELAND FOSTER WOOD, 20th-century American author, from *How Love
> Grows in Marriage*

All happiness or unhappiness solely depends upon the quality of the object to which we are attached by love. Love for an object eternal and infinite feeds the mind with joy alone, a joy that is free from all sorrow.

> —BARUCH SPINOZA, 17th-century Dutch philosopher

'Tis the gift to be simple
'Tis the gift to be free
'Tis the gift to come down
Where we ought to be

And when we find ourselves
In the place just right
It will be in the valley
Of love and delight.

> —FROM "Simple Gifts," a Shaker hymn

. . . when we find ourselves
Though the balmy air of night
    How they ring out their delight!
    From the molten golden notes,
    What a liquid ditty floats
To the turtle-dove that listens, while she gloats
    On the moon!
Oh, from out of the sounding cells,
What a gush of euphony voluminously wells!
    How it swells!
    How it dwells
    On the Future! How it tells
    Of the rapture that impels
To the swinging and the ringing
    Of the bells, bells, bells,
    Of the bells, bells, bells, bells,
To the rhyming and the chiming of the bells!

    –EDGAR ALLAN POE, 19th-century American writer, from "The Bells"

Serene will be our days and bright
And happy will our nature be,
When love is an unerring light,
And joy its own security.

    –WILLIAM WORDSWORTH, 18th-/19th-century poet, from *Ode to Duty*

When the one man loves the one woman and the one woman
loves the one man, the very angels desert heaven and come and
sit in that house and sing for joy.

    –*BRAHMA SUTRA,* an authoritative Hindu text

We cannot really love anybody with whom we never laugh.

—AGNES REPPLIER, 19th-/20th-century essayist

That is the best—to laugh with someone because you think the same things are funny.

—GLORIA VANDERBILT, 20th-century American fashion designer and socialite

The man and the woman who can laugh at their love, who can kiss with smiles and embrace with chuckles, will outlast in mutual affection all the throat-lumpy, cow-eyed couples of their acquaintance. Nothing lives on so fresh and evergreen as the love with a funny bone.

—GEORGE JEAN NATHAN, 20th-century American editor and drama critic

Love

Love one another and you will be happy. It's as simple and as difficult as that.

—MICHAEL LEUNIG, Australian cartoonist

Love is the same as like except you feel sexier.

—JUDITH VIORST, contemporary writer

Love is the joy of the good, the wonder of the wise, the amazement of the Gods.

—PLATO, ancient Greek philosopher

One word frees us of all the weight and pain of life: that word is love.

—SOPHOCLES, ancient Greek poet

No cord nor cable can so forcibly draw, or hold so fast, as love can do with a twined thread.

—ROBERT BURTON, 16th-/17th-century English author and clergyman

What is the beginning? Love.
What the course, Love still.
What the goal. The goal is Love.
On a happy hill
Is there nothing then but Love?
Search we sky or earth
There is nothing out of Love
Hath perpetual worth:
All things flag but only Love,
All things fail and flee,
There is nothing left but Love
Worth you and me.

—CHRISTINA ROSSETTI, 19th-century English poet, from "What Is the Beginning"

Can one have love? If we could, love would need to be a thing, a substance that one can have, own, possess. The truth is, there is no such thing as "love." "Love" is an abstraction, perhaps a goddess or an alien being, although nobody has ever seen this goddess . . . To say "I have a great love for you" is not a thing that one can have, but a process, an inner activity that one is the subject of. I can love, I can be in love, but in love I have nothing. In fact, the less I have the more I can love.

—ERICH FROMM, 20th-century American psychoanalyst, from *To Have or To Be*

A coward is incapable
of exhibiting love;

it is the prerogative
of the brave.

> –MAHATMA GANDHI, 20th-century Indian nationalist leader, the father of
> nonviolent resistance

Absence diminishes small loves and increases great ones, as the
wind blows out the candle and blows up the bonfire.

> –FRANÇOIS DE LA ROCHEFOUCAULD, 17th-century French writer, *Maxims
> and Reflections*

To love is to place our happiness in the happiness of another.

> –BARON GOTTFRIED VON LEIBNITZ, 16th-/17th-century German philosopher/
> mathematician

To love is to
admire with the heart;
to admire is to
love with the mind.

> –THÉOPHILE GAUTIER, 19th-century French author

Neither a lofty degree of intelligence nor imagination nor both
together go to the making of genius. Love, love, love, that is the
soul of genius.

> –WOLFGANG AMADEUS MOZART, 18th-century Austrian composer

When one has once fully entered the realm of love, the world—
no matter how imperfect—becomes rich and beautiful, it consists solely of opportunities for love.

> –SÖREN KIERKEGAARD, 19th-century Danish philosopher

Love looks through a telescope; envy, through a microscope.

–JOSH BILLINGS, 19th-century American humorist

You have to walk carefully in the beginning of love; the running across fields into your lover's arms can only come later when you're sure they won't laugh if you trip.

–JONATHAN CARROLL, contemporary American novelist, from *Outside the Dog Museum*

But love don't make things nice. It ruins everything. It breaks your heart. It makes things a mess.

–RONNY (ACTOR NICOLAS CAGE), in the movie *Moonstruck*

Love is a portion of the soul itself, and it is of the same nature as the celestial breathing of the atmosphere of paradise.

–VICTOR HUGO, 19th-century French dramatist, novelist and poet

Miracles occur naturally as expressions of love. The real miracle is the love that inspires them. In this sense everything that comes from love is a miracle.

–MARIANNE WILLIAMSON, contemporary American self-help guru and writer

In literature as in love, we are astonished at what is chosen by others.

–ANDRÉ MAUROIS, 20th-century French writer

The way to love anything is to realize that it might be lost.

–G. K. CHESTERTON, 19th-/20th-century writer

Love is a fire. But whether it is going to warm your hearth or burn down your house, you can never tell.

–JOAN CRAWFORD, American actress

From all the offspring
of the earth and heaven
love is the most precious.

–SAPPHO, Greek poet of the 7th-century, B.C.

It is with true love as it is with ghosts; everyone talks about it, but few have seen it.

–FRANÇOIS DE LA ROCHEFOUCAULD, 17th-century French writer, *Reflections and Maxims*

We cease loving ourselves if no one loves us.

–MME. DE STAËL, 19th-century French writer

Gravitation cannot be held responsible for people falling in love.

–ALBERT EINSTEIN, 20th-century Nobel prize–winning physicist

Love and work are the cornerstones of our humanness.

–SIGMUND FREUD, 19th-/20th-century father of psychoanalysis

We love because it's the only true adventure.

–NIKKI GIOVANNI, 20th-century American poet and essayist

If it is your time, love will track you down like a cruise missile.

–LYNDA BARRY, contemporary cartoonist and writer

Love, in the divine alchemy of life, transmutes all duties into privileges, all responsibilities into joys.

–WILLIAM GEORGE JORDAN, 19th-/20th-century motivational speaker

Love one human being purely and warmly, and you will love all . . . The heart in this heaven, like the sun in its course, sees nothing, from the dewdrop to the ocean, but a mirror which it brightens, and arms, and fills.

–Conrad Richter, 20th-century American novelist

It is the true season
of Love
when we know that
we alone can love;
that no one could ever
have loved before us
and that no one
will ever Love
in the same way
after us.

–Johann Wolfgang von Goethe, 18th-/19th-century German poet and
    dramatist

Hatred paralyzes life; love releases it.
Hatred confuses life; love harmonizes it.
Hatred darkens life; love illumines it,

–Martin Luther King, Jr., American civil rights leader

To love someone deeply gives you strength. Being loved by some-one deeply gives you courage.

–Lao Tzu, ancient Chinese philosopher

The bottom line is that (a) people are never perfect, but love can be, (b) that is the one and only way that the mediocre and vile can be transformed, and (c) doing that makes it that. We waste time looking for the perfect lover, instead of creating the perfect love.

–Tom Robbins, 20th-century American writer

Love gives us in a moment
what we can hardly attain
by effort after years of toil.

–Johann Wolfgang von Goethe, 18th-/19th-century German poet and dramatist

Love looks not with the eyes, but with the mind; And therefore is winged Cupid painted blind.

–William Shakespeare, 16th-/17th-century English poet and playwright, from *A Midsummer Night's Dream*

I have found the paradox that if I love until it hurts, then there is no hurt, but only more love.

– Mother Teresa, 20th-century Catholic missionary

Aristophanes: Love is the oldest of the gods, and he is also the source of the greatest benefits to us . . .

–Plato, ancient Greek philosopher, from the *Symposium*

Agathon: [Love is] the youngest of the gods and youthful ever.

–Plato, ancient Greek philosopher, from the *Symposium*

There is only
one terminal dignity—
love.
And the story of a love
is not important
what is important
is that one is capable of love.

It is perhaps the only glimpse
we are permitted of eternity.

> –HELEN HAYES, American actress

We can do not great things—only small things with great love.

> –MOTHER TERESA, 20th-century Catholic missionary

The first duty of love is to listen.

> –PAUL TILLICH, 19th-/20th-century German/American philosopher

Love means never having to say you're sorry.

> –OLIVER BARRETT (ACTOR RYAN O'NEAL), in the movie *Love Story*

Love. What small word we use for an idea so immense and powerful it has altered the flow of history, calmed monsters, kindled works of art, cheered the forlorn, turned tough guys to mush, consoled the enslaved, driven strong women mad, glorified the humble, fueled national scandals, bankrupted robber barons, and made mincemeat of kings. How can love's spaciousness be conveyed in the narrow confines of one syllable? . . . Love is an ancient delirium, a desire older than civilization, with taproots stretching deep into dark and mysterious days . . .

The heart is a loving museum. In each of its galleries, no matter how narrow or dimly lit, preserved forever like wondrous diatoms, are our moments of living and being loved.

> –DIANE ACKERMAN, contemporary American poet and writer, from *A Natural History of Love*

Love is a taste of paradise.

> –SHOLEM ALEICHEM, 20th-century Russian/American humorist

It feels like how love should be . . . floating through a dark blue sky.

—ANNA SCOTT (ACTRESS JULIA ROBERTS), in the movie *Notting Hill*

If you would be loved, love and be lovable.

—BENJAMIN FRANKLIN,18th-century American patriot, diplomat, author, printer, scientist and inventor

Infatuation is when you think that he's as sexy as Robert Redford, as smart as Henry Kissinger, as noble as Ralph Nader, as funny as Woody Allen, and as athletic as Jimmy Conners. Love is when you realize that he's as sexy as Woody Allen, as smart as Jimmy Conners, as funny as Ralph Nader, as athletic as Henry Kissinger, and nothing like Robert Redford—but you'll take him anyway.

—JUDITH VIORST, contemporary author

The test of a happily married—and a wise woman—is whether she can say, "I love you" far oftener than she asks "Do you love me?"

—DOROTHY DAYTON

Love—is anterior to Life—
Posterior—to Death—
Initial of creation, and
The Exponent of Earth.

—EMILY DICKINSON, 19th-century American poet, from *The Complete Poems*

We are all born for love; it is the principle of existence and its only end.

—BENJAMIN DISRAELI, 19th-century author and British prime minister

Love, then hath every bliss in store;
'Tis friendship and 'tis something more.
Each other every wish they give;
Not to know love is not to live.

–JOHN GAY, 17th-/18th-century English poet and dramatist

Who then can doubt that we exist only to love? Disguise it, in fact, as we will, we love without intermission. Where we seem most effectually to shut out love, it lies covert and concealed; we live not a moment exempt from its influence.

–BLAISE PASCAL, 17th-century French mathematician and philosopher, from his essay *On the Passion of the Soul*

Aristophanes: I believe that if our loves were perfectly accomplished, and each one returning to his primeval nature had his original true love, then our race would be happy . . . [Therefore] we must praise the god Love, who is our greatest benefactor, both leading us in this life back to our own nature, and giving us high hopes for the future, for he promises that if we are pious, he will restore us to our original state, and heal us, and make us happy and blessed.

–PLATO, ancient Greek philosopher, from the *Symposium*

The memories of long love
Gather like drifting snow,
Poignant as the mandarin ducks,
Who float side by side in sleep.

Falling from the ridge
Of high Tsukuba
The Minano River
At last gathers itself,

Like my love, into
A deep, still pool.

> –KENNETH REXROTH, 20th-century American poet, from *One Hundred Poems from the Japanese*

For one human being to love another; that is perhaps the most difficult of all our tasks, the ultimate, the last test and proof, the work for which all other work is but preparation.

> –RAINER MARIA RILKE, 19th-/20th-century German poet, from *Letters to a Young Poet,* translated by M. D. Herter Norton

There is no remedy for love than to love more.

> –HENRY DAVID THOREAU, 19th-century American writer

Love is blynd.

> –GEOFFREY CHAUCER, 14th-century British author of *The Canterbury Tales*

That love is all there is
Is all we know of love.

> –EMILY DICKINSON, 19th-century American poet

The only present love demands is love.

> –JOHN GAY, 17th-/18th-century English poet and dramatist

Love consists in this, that two solitudes protect and touch and greet each other.

> –RAINER MARIA RILKE, 19th-/20th-century German poet from *Letters to a Young Poet*

Agathon: [Love] walks . . . in the hearts and souls of both gods and men, which are of all things the softest: in them he walks and dwells and makes his home. Not in every soul without exception, for where there is hardness he departs, where there is softness there he dwells . . . he dwells in the place of flowers and scents, there he sits and abides . . .

–PLATO, ancient Greek philosopher, from the *Symposium*

Love doesn't make the world go round. Love is what makes the ride worthwhile.

–FRANKLIN JONES, humorist

A man is not where he lives, but where he loves.

–LATIN PROVERB

And this I pray, that your love may abound yet more and more in knowledge and in all judgement;
    That ye may approve things that are excellent.

–PHILIPPIANS 1:9–10, *The Holy Bible,* King James version

He who loves is a slave; he who is loved is a master.

–POLISH PROVERB

It is difficult to define love. But we may say that in the soul, it is a ruling passion; in the mind, it is a close sympathy and affinity; in the body, a wholly secret and delicate longing to possess what we love—and this after much mystery.

–FRANÇOIS DE LA ROCHEFOUCAULD, 17th-century French writer, *Reflections and Maxims*

Love, faithful love, recalled thee to my mind—

–WILLIAM WORDSWORTH, 18th-/19th-century poet

. . . love,
    the breaking
of your
    soul
    upon
my lips

–E. E. CUMMINGS, 20th-century American poet, from *Amores*

Together we stood without words
And love, like the heavy fragrance
Of the flowering thorn tree, pierced us

–GABRIELLA MISTRAL, 19th-/20th-century Chilean poet and educator, from
"God Wills It," translated by K.G.C.

Socrates: Human nature will not easily find a helper better than
love. And therefore I say that every man ought to honor him,
and walk in his ways and exhort others to do the same, and
praise the power and spirit of love . . . now and forever.

– PLATO, ancient Greek philosopher, from the *Symposium*

Not knowing what love is. It was in this condition that many
girls would marry once upon a time where we came from, they
would live their whole lives without knowing this sensation of
the soul, confusing it with respect, resignation, duty, habit. In the
end they would die without ever having felt its existence . . . the
sudden discovery of this sensation could be so shattering, that it
was destined to disrupt all things.

–TRANSLATION OF OPENING LINES of the Italian movie *The Best Man*

Marriage Itself

Marriage is a sea of dreams.

>   –FRANK CRANE, contemporary writer

. . . Still, I am prepared for this voyage, and for anything else you may care to mention.

>   –JOHN ASHBERRY, contemporary American poet, from *The Skaters*

Marriage is more than four bare legs in a bed.

>   –HOSHANG N. AKHTAR

Marriage has less beauty but more safety than the single life. It's full of sorrows and full of joys. It lives under more burdens, but it is supported by all the strength of love, and those burdens are delightful.

>   –CLOSING NARRATION in the movie *Forces of Nature*

The aim of marriage should be to give the best years of your life to the spouse who makes them the best.

>   –ANONYMOUS

The goal of our life should not be to find joy in marriage, but to bring more love and truth into the world. We marry to assist each other in this task.

>   –LEO TOLSTOY, 19th-century Russian novelist

Any marriage which is turned in upon itself, in which the bride and groom simply gaze obsessively at one another, goes out after a time.

A marriage which really works is one which works for others. Marriage has both a private face and a public importance. If we solved all our economic problems and failed to build loving families, it would profit us, nothing, because the family is the place where the future is created good and full of love—or deformed.

Those who are married live happily ever after the wedding day if they persevere in the real adventure, which is the royal task of creating each other and creating a more loving world.

–ARCHBISHOP OF CANTERBURY, on the marriage of Queen Elizabeth II

Marriage is that relationship between man and woman in which the independence is equal, the dependence mutual, and the obligation reciprocal.

–L. K. ANSPACHER, 19th-/20th-century American dramatist

The married man may bear his yoke with ease,
Secure at once himself and Heav'n to please;
And pass his inoffensive hours away,
In bliss all night, and innocence all day;
Tho' fortune change, his constant spouse remains,
Augments his joys, or mitigates his pains.

–ALEXANDER POPE, 18th-century English poet

The joys of marriage are the heaven on earth,
Life's paradise, great princess, the soul's quiet,
Sinews of concord, earthy immortality,
Eternity of pleasures.

–JOHN FORD, 16th-/17th-century English dramatist

You must marry, or your life will be wasted . . . You can transmute love, ignore it, muddle it, but you can never pull it out of you . . . When I think what life is, and how seldom love is answered by love—Marry him; it is one of the moments for which the world was made . . .

> –E. M. FORSTER, 19th-/20th-century English novelist, from *A Room with a View*

It's about time you got married before you turn into a lonesome, bitter old man.

> –STELLA (ACTRESS THELMA RITTER) TO JEFF (ACTOR JAMES STEWART), in the movie *Rear Window*

Marriage is the only known example of the happy meeting of the immovable object and the irresistible force.

> –OGDEN NASH, 20th-century American poet

Marriages are made in heaven, but they are lived on earth.

> –NATHAN H. GIST

We bachelors laugh and show our teeth, but you married men laugh till your hearts ache.

> –GEORGE HERBERT, 17th-century English poet

Just as it is the crown, and not merely the will to rule, that makes the king, so it is marriage, and not merely your love for each other, that joins you together in the sight of God and man. As high as God is above man, so high are the sanctity, the rights, and the promise of marriage above the sanctity, the rights and the promise of love. It is not your love that sustains marriage, but from now on, the marriage that sustains your love.

> –DIETRICH BONHOEFFER, 20th-century German Protestant theologian, from *Letters and Papers from Prison*

Loose though it be,
The joint is free;

So, when love's yoke is on,
It must not gall,
Nor fret at all,
    With hard oppression.

    –ROBERT HERRICK, 17th-century English poet, from "To Julia"

A married man forms married habits and becomes dependent on
marriage just as a sailor becomes dependent on the sea.

    –GEORGE BERNARD SHAW, 19th-/20th-century, Irish-born British playwright

Not caged, my bird, my shy, sweet bird,
But nested—nested!

    –HUBBERTON LULHAM

All I know for sure from seven years of marriage so far . . . is this:
a good marriage is worth more than rubies, flowers, flattery and
French perfume; a true, loving husband or wife is a passionate gift
from life. A bad marriage is hell on earth and more predatory and
dangerous to a person's body and soul than the thing from *Alien*.

    –ANNA MARIA DELL'OSO, contemporary Australian feminist writer

We; —
They; —
Small words, but mighty.
In their span
Are bound the life and hopes of man.
For them, life's best is centered round their love;
Till younger lives come all their love to prove.

    –JOHN OXENHAM, 19th-/20th-century English journalist and poet, from
    "The Little Poem of Life"

Marriage is a mistake every man should make.

    –GEORGE JESSEL, contemporary American comedian

I have yet to hear a man ask for advice on how to combine marriage and a career.

    –GLORIA STEINEM, contemporary American feminist

Rituals are important. Nowadays it's not hip to be married. I'm not interested in being hip.

    –JOHN LENNON, British singer/songerwriter, member of the rock group
    The Beatles

Of course I want to get married again. Who doesn't? It's the biggest thing you can do in life.

    –SHOTZIE (ACTRESS LAUREN BECALL) explaining the impetus behind her
    scheme to land herself a (rich) second husband, in the movie *How to
    Marry a Millionaire*

The only thing that can hallow marriage is love, and the only genuine marriage is that which is hallowed by love.

    –LEO TOLSTOY, 19th-century Russian novelist

Any marriage, happy or unhappy, is infinitely more interesting and significant than any romance, however passionate.

    –W. H. AUDEN, 20th-century, English-born American poet.

thigh and tongue, beloved,
are heavy with it,
it throbs in the teeth . . .

We look for communion
and are turned away, beloved,
each and each

It is leviathan and we
in its belly

looking for joy, some joy
not be known outside it

two by two in the ark of
the ache of it.

> —DENISE LEVERTOV, 20th-century American poet, from "The Ache of
> Marriage"

Marriage is a sweet state,
I can affirm it by my own experience,
In a very truth, I who have a good and wise husband
Whom God helped me to find.
I give thanks to him who will save him for me,
For I can truly feel his great goodness
And for sure the sweet man loves me well.

Throughout that first night in our home,
I could well feel his great goodness,
For he did me no excess
That could hurt me.
But before it was time to get up,
He kissed me 100 times, this I affirm,
Without exacting further outrage,
And yet for sure sweet man loves me well.

> —CHRISTINE DE PISAN, 14th-/15th-century French poet and historian, from
> "In Praise of Marriage"

It is easier to be a lover than a husband for the simple reason that
it is more difficult to be witty every day than to produce the occasional bon mot.

> —HONORÉ DE BALZAC, 19th-century French novelist, *Physiologie du Mariage*

The first bond of society is marriage.

> —CICERO, 1st-century, B.C. Roman statesman

. . . [M]arriage is not to be entered into unadvisedly or lightly, but reverently, deliberately, and in accordance with the purposes for which it was instituted by God.

–From "The Celebration and Blessing of a Marriage" in *The Book of Common Prayer*

When I look back now I can't understand what women like Liz Taylor have been doing all these years. I have feelings of immense relief that I got it all over and done with in such a short space of time. Imagine dedicating your entire life to the pursuit of marriage. No wonder Liz has battled booze, drugs, diets, surgery and pills for so long—she has been driven to them.

–Jan Owen, contemporary Australian author

A successful marriage requires falling in love many times always with the same person.

–Mignon McLaughlin, contemporary writer

MARRIAGE, n. The state or condition of a community consisting of a master, a mistress and two slaves, making in all, two.

–Ambrose Bierce, 19th-/20th-century American writer, from *The Devil's Dictionary*

Marriage is an adventure, like going to war.

–G. K. Chesterton, 19th-/20th-century writer

Love is an ideal thing, marriage a real thing; a confusion of the real with the ideal never goes unpunished.

–Johann Wolfgang von Goethe, 18th-/19th-century German poet and dramatist

Thank heaven. A bachelor's life is no life for a single man.

–Samuel Goldwyn, American immigrant-turned-famous-movie-producer, when told his son was getting married

Marriage is a great institution, but I'm not ready for an institution yet.

—MAE WEST, American actress

Love and marriage are two goals approached by different and distinct paths . . . Marriage has utility, justice, honor and constancy for its share . . . Love builds itself wholly upon pleasure . . . Marriage is a solemn and religious tie; and therefore the pleasure we take from it should be restrained, serious and seasoned with a certain gravity . . . That few are observed to be happy is a token of its value and price. If well-formed and rightly taken, there is not a finer estate in human society. Though we cannot live without it, yet we do nothing but decry it. We see the same with bird-cages: the birds outside despair to get in and those within despair to get out.

—MICHEL DE MONTAIGNE, 16th-century French essayist, from *The Auto-biography*

Partnership, Friendship And Companionship

And yet even while I was exulting in my solitude I became aware of a strange lack. I wished a companion to lie near me in the starlight silent and not moving, but ever within touch. For there is a fellowship more quiet even than solitude, and which, rightly understood, is solitude made perfect. And to live out of doors with the woman a man loves is of all lives the most complete and free.

> –ROBERT LOUIS STEVENSON, 19th-century Scottish author, from *A Night Among the Pines*

Marriage is a partnership
in which each inspires the other,
and brings fruition to both.

> –MILLICENT CAREY MCINTOSH

To love means to decide independently to live with an equal partner, and to subordinate oneself to the formation of a new subject, a "we."

> –FRITZ KUNKEL, contemporary psychological theologian

The one word above all others that makes marriage successful is "ours."

> –ROBERT QUILLEN

There is no place like a bed for confidential disclosures between friends. Man and wife, they say, there open the very bottom of their souls to each other; and some old couples often lie and chat over old times till nearly morning.

> –HERMAN MELVILLE, 19th-century American writer, known for *Moby Dick*

Ultimately, the bond of all companionship, whether in marriage or in friendship, is conversation.

> –OSCAR WILDE, 19th-century Irish author and playwright

Married couples who love each other tell each other a thousand things without talking.

–CHINESE PROVERB

Marriage must exemplify friendship's highest ideal . . .

–MARGARET E. SANGER, 20th-century women's rights activist

Love may be the spark that started the flame, but friendship is the timber that keeps it burning.

–TONY JONES (ACTOR BRAD MAULE) to his TV wife, Bobbie Spencer (ACTRESS JACKLYN ZEMAN), in the daytime drama *General Hospital,* in 1985

A good marriage is based on the talent for friendship.

–FRIEDRICH NIETZSCHE, 19th-century German philosopher

If there is such a thing as a good marriage, it is because it resembles friendship rather than love.

–MICHEL DE MONTAIGNE, 16th-century French essayist, from *The Autobiography*

There are three great friends: an old wife, an old dog, and ready money.

–BENJAMIN FRANKLIN, 18th-century American patriot, diplomat, author, printer, scientist and inventor

Only choose in marriage
   A woman
whom you would choose

As a friend
if she were a man.

> –Joseph Joubert, 18th-/19th-century French essayist

I can't think of a better way to get through this life than with
your best friend. It's a place where those loving feelings that we
have can be nurtured. And can flower and bloom. You see, when
friends become lovers and then husbands and wives, well, two is
definitely better than one, to themselves and to everyone they
touch.

> –Lee Baldwin (Peter Hansen) to his TV son, Scott (Kin Shriner),
> before Scott's wedding, on the daytime TV drama *General Hospital,*
> 1993

She who dwells with me, who I have loved
With such communion, that no place on earth
Can ever be a solitude for me.

> –William Wordsworth, 18th-/19th-century poet

The real test of friendship is: Can you literally do nothing with
the other person? Can you enjoy together those moments of
life that are utterly simple? They are the moments people look
back on at the end of life and number as their most sacred expe-
riences.

> –Eugene Kennedy

The secret of a happy marriage is simple: Just keep on being as
polite to one another as you are to your best friends.

> –Robert Quillen

Thus hand in hand through life—we'll go;
Its checkered paths of joy and woe
With cautious steps we'll tread.

> –NATHANIEL COTTON 18th-century poet, from *Early Thoughts of Marriage*

Take my hand. There are two of us in this cave.

> –LISEL MUELLER, German-born contemporary poet, from "The Blind Leading the Blind"

There is nothing better in this world than that man and woman, sharing the same ideas, keep house together. It discomforts their enemies and makes the hearts of their friends glad—but they themselves know more about it than anyone.

> –HOMER, ancient Greek poet, from *The Odyssey*

Teacher, tender comrade, wife,
A fellow-farer true through life.

> –ROBERT LOUIS STEVENSON, Scottish 19th-century author

". . . Dear beast, you shall not die," said Beauty. "You will live in order to become my husband. From this moment on I give you my hand and I swear that I shall be yours alone. Alas! I thought that I felt only friendship for you, but the sorrow that I feel now makes me see that I cannot live without you."

> –MADAME LEPRINCE DE BEAUMONT, 18th-century French writer, from *Beauty and the Beast*

Love does not consist in gazing at each other but in looking outward together in the same direction. There is no comradeship except through union in the same high effort.

> –ANTOINE DE SAINT-EXUPERY, 20th-century French writer

Marriage is to think together.

> –ROBERT C. DODDS, from *Two Together: A Handbook for Your Marriage*

Your life and my life flow into each other as wave flows into wave, and unless there is peace and joy and freedom for you, there can be no real peace or joy or freedom for me. To see reality—not as we expect it to be but as it is—is to see that unless we live for each other and in and through each other, we do not really live very satisfactorily; that there can really be life only where there really is, in just this sense, love.

> –FREDERICK BUECHNER, contemporary American novelist, preacher and essayist, from *The Magnificent Defeat*

I do . . . And I also wash and iron them.

> –DENNIS THATCHER, husband of 20th-century British Prime Minister Margaret Thatcher, when asked who wore the pants in his family

You jump, I jump, remember? I can't turn away without knowing you'll be all right.

> –JACK (ACTOR LEONARDO DICAPRIO) to ROSE (ACTRESS KATE WINSLET), in the movie *Titanic*

When two people love each other, they don't look at each other, they look in the same direction.

> –GINGER ROGERS, actress/dancer known for dancing with Fred Astaire

No matter what comes down, it's you and me, pal, together.

> –ACTRESS KIM BASINGER, commenting on her marriage to actor Alec Baldwin

Socrates: Love begins with the desire of union.

> –PLATO, ancient Greek philosopher, from the *Symposium*

Marriage resembles a pair of shears, so joined that they cannot be separated; often moving in opposite directions, yet always punishing anyone who comes between them.

–SYDNEY SMITH, 18th-/19th-century English writer and clergyman

Whoever says marriage is a fifty-fifty proposition doesn't know the half of it.

–ANONYMOUS

You are holding up a ceiling
with both arms. It is very heavy,
but you must hold it up, or else
it will fall down on you. Your arms
are tired, terribly tired,
and as the day goes on, it feels
as if either your arms or the ceiling
will soon collapse.

But then,
unexpectedly,
something wonderful happens:
Someone,
a man or a woman,
walks into the room
and holds their arms up
to the ceiling beside you.

So you finally get
to take down your arms.
You feel the relief of respite,
the blood flowing back
to your fingers and arms.
And when your partner's arms tire,

you hold up your own
to relieve him again.

And it can go on like this
for many years
without the house falling.

> –MICHAEL BLUMENTHAL, contemporary American poet and essayist, from
> "A Marriage"

Here all seeking is over,
the lost has been found,
a mate has been found
to share the chills of winter—
now Love asks
that you be united.
Here is a place to rest,
a place to sleep,
a place in heaven.
Now two are becoming one,
the black night is scattered,
the eastern sky grows bright.
At last the great day has come!

> –HAWAIIAN SONG

Well-married a man is winged; ill-matched, he is shackled.

> –HENRY WARD BEECHER, 19th-century American clergyman

When to the session of sweet silent thought
I summon up remembrance of things past,
I sigh the lack of many a thing I sought,
And with old woes new wail my dear times' waste:
Then can I drown an eye, unus'd to flow,
For precious friends hid in death's dateless night,

And weep afresh love's long since cancell'd woe,
And moan the expense of many a vanish'd sight:
Then can I grieve at grievances oregone,
And heavily from woe to woe tell o'er
The sad account of fore-bemoaned moan,
Which I new pay as if not aid before.
But if the while I think on thee, dear friend,
All losses are restor'd and sorrows end.

> –WILLIAM SHAKESPEARE, 16th-/17th-century English poet and playwright,
> Sonnet XXX

I believe there is . . . an opportunity for the best relationship of all: not a limited, mutually exclusive one . . . and not a functional, dependent one . . . but the meeting of two whole, fully developed people as persons . . .

> –ANNE MORROW LINDBERGH, 20th-century American writer and the wife
> of aviator Charles Lindbergh, from *Gift from the Sea*

Marriage is a matter of give and take, but so far I haven't been able to find anybody who'll take what I have to give.

> –CASS DALEY, 20th-century American actress and comedian

Once the realization is accepted that even between the *closest* human beings infinite distances continue to exist, a wonderful living side by side can grow up, if they succeed in loving the distance between them which makes it possible for each to see each other whole against the sky.

> –RAINER MARIA RILKE, 19th-/20th-century German poet, from *Letters to a
> Young Poet*

The light of love
Shines over all,

Of love, that says
Not mine and thine,
But ours, for ours
Is thine and mine.

> –HENRY WADSWORTH LONGFELLOW, 19th-century American poet

Let us be guests in one another's house
With deferential "No" and courteous "Yes";
Let us take care to hide our foolish moods
Behind a certain show of cheerfulness.

Let us avoid all sullen silences;
We should find fresh and sprightly things to say;
I must be fearful lest you find me dull,
And you must dread to bore me any way.

Let us knock gently at each other's heart,
Glad of a chance to look within—and yet
Let us remember that to force one's way
Is the unpardoned breach of etiquette.

So shall I be hostess—you, the host—
Until all need for entertainment ends;
We shall be lovers when the last door shuts,
But what is better still—we shall be friends.

> –CAROL HAYNES, from the poem "Any Husband or Wife"

On the way to the airport after the wedding, the bride asked her husband, a bachelor for forty years, if he had their plane tickets. He confidently reached into his pocket . . . and then saw that out of habit, he had bought just one ticket. "Incredible! Just one ticket. You know, dear, I've been married only an hour and already I've forgotten about myself."

> –ANONYMOUS

Marriage has too often been portrayed as two people frozen together side by side, as immobile as marble statues. More accurately, it is the intricate and graceful cooperation of two dancers who through long practice have learned to match each other's movements and moods in response to the music of the spheres.

–DAVID R. MACE, 20th-century Scottish sociologist

I could open the doors
and the windows
to great winds.
let everything be scattered
like
loose
sheets of paper.
let tumbling take sense and
proportion from what we have
put in order
that suits us.
but it would not change
anything.
but it would not change
anything.
You have come in,
And your entrance
has been final.
You do not leave me,
nor do I leave you, beloved.
We have made of this house
our place
and our shelter.
When we go out, we will go out
together.

–TED ENSLIN, contemporary poet, from "The Place Poem–3"

... the greatest of all the arts is the art of living together ...

> –William Lyon Phelps, 19th-/20th-century American writer, critic and
> educator

This is my beloved and this is my friend ...

> –Song of Solomon 5:16, *The Holy Bible,* King James version

I've often wished to have a friend
With whom my choicest hours to spend,
To whom I safely may impart
Each wish and weakness of my heart.
Who would in every sorrow cheer,
And mingle with my grief a tear,
And to secure that bliss for life,
I'd like that friend to be my wife.

> –"The Wish," a verse from a Victorian card

Heart reposes upon heart with perfect confidence, and love unutterable, secure of a return of its warmest feelings. Unite! in the most perfect friendship.

> –from *Godey's Lady's Book,* a Victorian-era publication

There are three sights which warm my heart and are beautiful in the eyes of the Lord and of men: concord among brothers, friendship among neighbors, and a man and a wife who are inseparable.

> –from *The Wisdom of Ben Sira,* Chapter 25, Verse I

If love were what the rose is
    And I were like the leaf,
Our lives would grow together
In sad or singing weather,
Blown fields or flowerful closes,

Green pleasure or grey grief;
If love were what the rose is,
    And I were like the leaf.

> —ALGERNON CHARLES SWINBURNE, 19th-/20th-century English poet, from
> "A Match"

Passion

To start love like this: with the shot of a gun
Like Ramadan.

> —YEHUDA AMICHAI, German-born Israeli poet, from "Ideal Love"

When a man and a woman see each other and like each other,
they oughta come together. WHAM! Like a couple of taxis on
Broadway, not sit around analyzing each other like two speci-
mens in a bottle.

> —STELLA (ACTRESS THELMA RITTER), in the movie *Rear Window*

Passionate love relentlessly twists a cord
Under my heart and spreads deep mist on my eyes,
stealing the unguarded brains from my head.

> —ARCHILOCHOS, Greek poet of the 8th-century, B.C.

But, to the charms which I adore,
'Tis religion to be true!

> —RICHARD BRINSLEY SHERIDAN, 18th-/19th-century Irish dramatist

The absolute yearning of one human body for another particular
body and its indifference to substitutes is one of life's major
mysteries.

> —IRIS MURDOCH, 20th-century English novelist

In melody divine,
My heart it beats to rapturous love,
I long to call you mine.

    —FROM A VICTORIAN CARD

God will not give you the light
Unless you walk by my side.
God will not let you drink
If I do not tremble in the water.
He will not let you sleep
Except in the hollow of my hair.

    —GABRIELLA MISTRAL, 19th-/20th-century Chilean poet and educator, from
    "God Wills It"

In endowing us with memory, nature has revealed to us a truth
utterly unimaginable to the unreflective creation, the truth of immortality . . . The most ideal human passion is love, which is
also the most absolute and animal and one of the most
ephemeral.

    —GEORGE SANTAYANA, 19th-/20th-century American philosopher, from
    Reason in Religion

Under the influence of strong passion the beloved object seems
new in every interview. Absence instantaneously creates a void
in the heart. Then, the joys of reunion.

    —BLAISE PASCAL, 17th-century French mathematician and philosopher,
    from *On the Passion of the Soul*

. . . our love it was strong by far than the love
Of those who were older than we
Of many far wiser than we—
And so, all the night-tide, I lie down by the side
Of my darling, my darling, my life and my bride . . .

    —EDGAR ALLAN POE, 19th-century American writer, from "Annabel Lee"

Scott—there's nothing in all the world I want but you—and your precious love—All material things are nothing . . . and I'd do anything—anything—to keep your heart for my own—I don't want to live—I want to love first and live incidentally . . . Don't you think I was made for you? I feel like you had me ordered—and I was delivered to you.

> –ZELDA SAYRE, 20th-century American writer, to her husband, writer F. Scott Fitzgerald, author of *The Great Gatsby*

Charles is life itself
pure life force, like sunlight—
and it is for this that I
married him and this is
what holds me to him—
caring always,
caring desperately

what happens to him and
whatever he happens
to be involved in.

> –ANNE MORROW LINDBERGH, 20th-century American writer and the wife of aviator Charles Lindbergh

The passion which unites the sexes . . . is habitually spoken of as though it were a simple feeling; whereas it is the most compound, and therefore the most powerful, of all the feelings.

> –HERBERT SPENCER, 19th-/20th-century philosopher, from *The Principles of Psychology*

"She's my girl . . . She's my blue sky. After sixteen years, I still bite her shoulders. She makes me feel like Hannibal crossing the Alps."

> –JOHN CHEEVER, 20th-century American writer, from his short story "The Country Husband"

I know not whether thou has been absent:
I lie down with thee, I rise up with thee,
In my dreams thou are with me.
If my eardrops tremble in my ears,
I know it is thou moving within my heart.

    –AZTEC LOVE SONG

Sex

I was promised sex. Everybody said it. You be a bridesmaid, you
get sex. You'll be fighting them off.

    –BRIDESMAID LYDIA (ACTRESS SOPHIE THOMPSON), complaining about a lack
    of wedding-party action, in the movie *Four Weddings and a Funeral*

The Sun-beams in the East are spred,
Leave, leave faire Bride, your solitary bed,
No more shall you returne to it alone,
It nourseth sadnesse, and your bodies print,
Like to a grave, the yielding downe doth dint;
You and your other you meet the anon;
Put forth, put forth that warme balm-breathing thigh,
Which when next time you in these sheets will smother,
There it must meet another . . .
Come glad from thence, goe gladder than you came,
Today put on perfection and a womans name . . .

    –JOHN DONNE, 16th/17th-century English poet and clergyman, from
    "Epithalamion Made at Lincoln's Inn"

Wild Nights—Wild Nights!
Were I with thee
Wild Nights should be
Our luxury!

Futile—the Winds—
To a Heart in port
Done with the Compass—
Done with the Chart!

Rowing in Eden—
Ah, the Sea!
Might I but moor—Tonight—
In Thee!

> –EMILY DICKINSON, 19th-century American poet, from *The Complete Poems,* edited by Thomas H. Johnson

The canopy is the cover of our bed
where our bodies open their portals wide,
where we eat and drink the blood
of our love, where the skin shines red
as a swallowed sunrise and we burn
in one furnace of joy molten as steel
and the dreams is fresh and flower.

> –MARGE PIERCY, feminist writer, "The Chuppah," June 2, 1982, on her marriage to Ira Wood

Who will plow my body?
Who will plow my high field?
Who will plow my wet ground?

Who will station the ox there?
Who will plow my body?

Great Lady, the King will plow your body.
I the King will plow your body.

> —From an ancient Sumerian sacred-wedding poem, adapted from the translation by Diane Wolkstein and Samuel Noah Kramer

Come now
    to your
bedroom to your
bed
    and play there
sweetly   gently
with your bridegroom . . .

> —SAPPHO, Greek poet of the 7th-century, B.C.

The best way to hold a man is in your arms.

> —MAE WEST, American actress

Love is the answer, but while you're waiting for the answer, sex raises some pretty good questions.

> —WOODY ALLEN, 20th-century American humorist, writer and filmmaker

ARDOR, n. The quality that distinguishes love without knowledge.

> —AMBROSE BIERCE, 19th-/20th-century American writer, from *The Devil's Dictionary*

Anyone can be passionate, but it takes real lovers to be silly.

> —ROSE FRANKEN, 20th-century American author and playwright

Marriage is popular because it combines the maximum of temptation with the maximum of opportunity.

> –GEORGE BERNARD SHAW, 20th-century American author and playwright

I married the first man I ever kissed. When I tell this to my children they just about throw up.

> –BARBARA BUSH, wife of 41st U.S. president, George Bush

One cardinal rule of marriage should never be forgotten: "Give little, give seldom, and above all, give grudgingly." Otherwise, what could have been a proper marriage could become an orgy of sexual lust.

> –RUTH SMYTHERS, from *Marriage Advice for Women,* 1894

I rely on my personality for birth control.

> –LIZ WINSTON, contemporary comedian

I hear if you have fertility dolls, you don't need Viagara.

> –JESSE JACKSON, JR., congressman and son of Reverend Jesse Jackson, commenting of his wife's favorite wedding gift

The virgin's girdle now untie,
And in thy nuptiall bed (love's altar) lye
A pleasing sacrifice; now dispossesse
Thee of these chaines and robes which were put on
T'adorne the day, not thee, for thou, alone,
Like vertue'and truth, art best in nakedness;
This bed is onely to virginite
A grave, but, to a better state, a cradle;
Till now thou wast bout able

To be what now thou art; then that by thee
No more be said, I may bee, but, I am,
To night put on perfection and a womans name . . .

> –JOHN DONNE, 16th-/17th-century English poet and clergyman, from
> "Epithalamion Made at Lincoln's Inn"

So long as the emotional feelings between the couple are right,
so long as there is mutual trust and love, their bodies will invari-
ably make the appropriate responses.

> –DAVID R. MACE, 20th-century Scottish sociologist

Let him kiss me with the kisses of his mouth:
For thy love is better than wine . . .

> –SONG OF SOLOMON, 1:2, *The Holy Bible*, King James version

How fair is thy love, my sister, my spouse!
how much better is thy love than wine!

> –SONG OF SOLOMON, 4:10, *The Holy Bible,* King James version

How could I, blest with thee, long nights employ.
And how with thee the longest day enjoy!

> –TIBULLUS, 1st-century, B.C. Roman poet

Off with that girdle, like heavens zone glistering,
But a farre fairer world encompassing.
Unpin that spangled brest-plate, which you weare,
That the eyes of busy fooles may be stopt there:
Unlace your selfe, for that harmonious chime
Tells me from you that now 'tis your bed time.

. . . Licence my roving hands, and let them goe
Behind, before, above, between, below.
Oh my America, my new found lande,
My kingdome, safeliest when with one man mand'd . . .

> –JOHN DONNE, 16th-/17th-century English poet and clergyman, from,
> "Elegie XIX: To His Mistris Going to Bed"

Contraceptives should be used on every conceivable occasion.

> –SPIKE MILLIGAN, British comic

I want to tell you a terrific story about oral contraception. I asked
this girl to sleep with me and she said, "No."

> –WOODY ALLEN, 20th-century American humorist, writer and filmmaker

Marriage has many pains, but celibacy has no pleasures.

> –SAMUEL JOHNSON, English dictionary inventor/lexicographer, from
> "Rasselas"

Marriage may often be a story lake, but celibacy is almost always a muddy horsepond.

> –THOMAS LOVE PEACOCK, 19th-century English author and poet

So "celibacy is the highest state!" And why? Because "it is the
safest and easiest road to heaven?" A pretty reason . . . I should
have thought that that was a sign of a lower state and not a
higher. Noble spirits show their nobleness by daring the most
difficult paths. And even if marriage was but one weed-field of
temptations, as these miserable pedants say, who have either
never tried it, or misused it to their own shame, it would be a

greater deed to conquer its temptations than to flee from them in cowardly longings after ease and safety!

–DIALOGUE from an unknown 19th-century novel

The amorous evening starre is rose,
Why then should not our amorous starre inclose
Her selfe in her wishe'd bed? . . . all toyl'd beasts
Rest duly; at night all their toyles are dispensed;
But in their beds commenced
Are other labours, and more dainty feasts;
She goes a maid, who lest she turn the same
To night put on perfection and a womans name.

–JOHN DONNE, 16th-/17th-century English poet and clergyman, from "Epithalamion Made at Lincoln's Inn"

Soul Mates / Synergy

. . . he's more myself than I am. Whatever our souls are made of his and mine are the same . . . If all else perished and *he* remained, I should still continue to be, and if all else remained, and he was annihilated, the universe would turn to a might stranger . . . He's always, always in my mind; not as a pleasure to myself, but as my own being.

–EMILY BRONTË, 19th-century English writer, from *Wuthering Heights*

The union of souls will ever be more perfect than of bodies.

–ERASMUS, 15th-/16th-century Dutch religious scholar

My heart, I fain would ask thee
What then is Love? Say on.
"Two souls with but a single thought,
Two hearts that beat as one."

> —Josef von Munch-Bellinghausen, 19th-century German playwright and
> poet

There is no you, no I, no tomorrow,
No yesterday, no names, the truth of two
In a single body, a single soul,
Oh total being . . .

> —Octavio Paz, 20th-century Mexican poet and critic, from "Sunstone"

Bone of my bones, and flesh of my flesh.

> —Genesis 2:23, *The Holy Bible,* King James version

Flesh of my flesh, bone of my bone,
I here, thou there, yet both but one.

> —Anne Bradstreet, 17th-century American poet, from "A Letter to Her
> Husband, Absent Upon Public Employment"

So we grew together, like to a double cherry, seeming parted,
but yet no union in partition; two lovely berries bolded on one
stem.

> —William Shakespeare, 16th-/17th-century English poet and playwright,
> in *A Midsummer Night's Dream*

What greater thing is there for two human souls than to feel that
they are joined for life, to strengthen each other in all labor, to

rest on each other in all sorrow, to minister to each other in all pain, to be one with each other in silent unspeakable memories at the moment of the last parting?

—GEORGE ELIOT, 19th-century English novelist, from *Adam Bede*

The Fountains mingle with the River
    And the Rivers with the Oceans,
The Winds of Heaven mix forever
    With a sweet emotion;
Nothing in the world is single;
    All things by a law divine
In one spirit meet and mingle,
    Why not I with thine?—

See the mountains kiss high Heaven
    And the waves clasp one another,
No sister-flower would be forgiven
    If it disdained its brother,
And the sunlight clasps the earth
    And the moonbeams kiss the sea:
What is all this sweet work worth
    If thou kiss not me?

—PERCY BYSSHE SHELLEY, 19th-century English romantic poet from "Loves Philosophy"

Aristophanes: Original human nature was not like the present but different. The sexes were not two as they are now but originally three in number; there was a man, woman, and the union of the two . . . The man was originally the child of the sun, the woman of the earth, and the man-woman of the moon, which is made up of sun and earth . . . [Now] when one of them meets his other half, the actual half of himself, the pair are lost in an amazement of love and friendship and intimacy . . . These are the people who pass their whole lives together . . . The reason is that human nature was originally one and we were a whole, and the desire and pursuit of the whole is called love . . .

—PLATO, ancient Greek philosopher, from the *Symposium*

I hereby give myself. I love you. You are the only being whom I can love absolutely with my complete self, with all my flesh and mind and heart. You are my mate, my perfect partner, and I am yours. You must feel this now, as I do . . . It was a marvel that we ever met. It is some kind of divine luck that we are together now. We must never, never part again. We are, here in this, necessary beings, like gods. As we look at each other we verify, we know, the perfection of our love, we recognize each other. Here is my life, here if need be is my death.

—IRIS MURDOCH, 20th-century English novelist, from *The Book and the Brotherhood*

I am the sky. You are the earth. We are the earth and sky, united.

—BENEDICTION RECITED BY A HINDU GROOM REPRESENTING LORD SHIVA, creator and destroyer of the world, to his bride, who represents Lord Shiva's wife Parvati, during their wedding ceremony

. . . Do not live without me. Let us share the joys. We are word and meaning, united. You are thought and I am sound.

—FROM THE HINDU MARRIAGE RITUAL OF "SEVEN STEPS"

It is wrong to think that love comes from long companionship and persevering courtship. Love is the offspring of spiritual affinity and unless that affinity is created in a moment, it will not be created for years or even generations.

—KHALIL GIBRAN, 19th-/20th-century Lebanese poet and writer

Love is not a union merely between two creatures—it is a union between two spirits.

—FREDERICK W. ROBERTSON

But happy they, the happiest of their kind,
Whom gentler stars unite, and in one fate,
Their hearts, their fortunes, and their beings blend.

—JAMES THOMSON, 18th-century Scottish poet

God has set the type of marriage everywhere throughout creation . . . Every creature seeks its perfection in another . . . The very heavens and earth picture it to us.

—JOHN MILTON, 17th-century English poet

He is the half part of a blessed man,
Left to be finished by such a she;
And she a fair divided excellence,
Whose fullness of perfection lies in him.

—WILLIAM SHAKESPEARE, 16th-/17th-century English poet and playwright

Sweet be the glances we exchange, our faces showing true concord. Enshrine me in thy heart, and let a single spirit dwell within us.

—FROM THE ATHARVAVEDA, a collection of hymns, magic spells and incantations in Sanskrit verse, composed around 1500–1200 B.C.

Our state cannot be severed; we are one,
One flesh; to lose thee were to lose myself.

—JOHN MILTON, 17th-century English poet

Then blend they, like green leaves with golden flowers,
Somewhere there waiteth in this world of ours

For one lone soul, another lonely soul.
Each choosing each through all the weary hours,
And meeting strangely at one sudden goal,
into one beautiful perfect whole;
And life's long night is ended, and the way
Lies open onward to eternal day.

> –EDWIN ARNOLD, 19th-/20th-century English poet

From every human being there rises a light that reaches straight
to heaven. And when two souls that are destined to be together
find each other, their streams of light flow together, and a single
brighter light goes forth from their united being.

> –BAAL SHEM TOV, 18th-century Jewish mystic

You and I
Have so much love
That it
Burns like a fire,
In which we bake a lump of clay
Molded into a figure of you
And a figure of me,
Then we take both of them,
And mix the pieces with water,
and break them into pieces,
And mold again a figure of you,
And a figure of me.
I am in your clay.
You are in my clay.
In life we share a single quilt.
In death we will share one bed.

> –KUAN TAO-SHENG, 13th-/14th-century Chinese poet and painter

TO HAVE AND TO HOLD

Two happy lovers make one single bread . . .

> –PABLO NERUDA, 20th-century Chilean poet, Sonnet XLVIII

Two such as you, with such a master speed
Cannot be parted nor be swept away
From one another once you are agreed
That life is only life forevermore
Together wing to wing and oar to oar.

> –ROBERT FROST, 20th-century American poet, from "The Master Speed"

My true love hath my heart and I have his,
By just exchange one for another given;
I hold this dear and mine he cannot miss;
There never was a better bargain driven:
My true love hath my heart and I have his.

My heart in me keeps him and me in one;
My heart in him his thoughts and senses guides;
He loves my heart for once it was his own;
I cherish his because in me it bides:
My true love hath my heart and I have his.

> –SIR PHILIP SIDNEY, 16th-century English poet and statesman, from "My
> True Love Hath My Heart"

Let them into one another sink
so as to endure each other outright.

> –RAINER MARIA RILKE, 20th-century German writer and poet, from his
> poem "The Lovers"

Best image of myself and dearer half.

> –JOHN MILTON, 17th-century English poet, from *Paradise Lost, Book V*

You are the sea, I am a fish . . .

> –JALĀL AL-DĪN RŪMĪ, 13th-century Persian poet

As wing to bird,
water to fish
life to the living—
so you to me.

> –VIDYPATI, Hindu love poem, translated by Edward C. Dimock, Jr., and
> Denise Levertov

Marriage is the fusion
   Of two hearts
   the union of two lives—
   the coming together of two tributaries.

> –PETER MARSHALL, contemporary American author and theological
> historian

If ever were one, then surely we.
If ever man were lov'd by wife, then thee;
If ever wife was happy in a man,
Compare with me ye women if you can.
I prize thy love more than whole Mines of gold,
Or all the riches that the East doth hold.
My love is such that Rivers cannot quench,
Nor ought but love from thee, give recompence.
Thy love is such I can no way repay,
The heavens reward thee manifold I pray.
Then while we live, in love let's so persever,
That we when live no more, we may live ever.

> –ANNE BRADSTREET, 17th-century American poet, from "To My Dear and
> Loving Husband"

Man cannot find his satisfactions within himself only; and, as love is essential to him, he must seek the objects of his affection in external objects ... Such is the largeness of his heart, that it must be something resembling himself, and approximating to his own qualities. That kind of beauty, therefore, which satisfies man, must not only contribute to his enjoyment but partake of his own resemblance.

–BLAISE PASCAL, 17th-century French mathematician and philosopher, from *On the Passion of the Soul*

If two stand shoulder to shoulder against the gods,
Happy together, the gods themselves are helpless
Against them while they stand so.

–MAXWELL ANDERSON, 20th-century American dramatist and philosopher

Marriage: that I call the will of two to create the one who is more than those who created it.

–FRIEDRICH NIETZSCHE, 19th-century German philosopher

When two people are at one in their inmost hearts, they shatter even the strength of iron or of bronze.

–FROM THE *I CHING,* classic Chinese book of divination and fortune-telling

Two are better than one; because they have a good reward for their labour.

For if they fall, the one will lift up his fellow: but woe to him that is alone when he falleth; for he hath not another to help him up.

Again, if the two lie together, then they have heat: but how can one be warm alone?

–ECCLESIASTES 4:9–11, *The Holy Bible*, King James version

Where they create dreams,
There were not enough for both of us,
So we saw the same one . . .

–ANNA AKHMATOVA, 19th-/20th-century poet, from "Instead of an After-word"

It is the man and woman united that make the complete human being. Together they are most likely to succeed in the world.

–BENJAMIN FRANKLIN, 18th-century American patriot, diplomat, author, printer, scientist and inventor

I can't do everything myself,
Mysterious is the fusion of two loving spirits; each takes the best from the other, but only to give it back again enriched with love.

–ROMAIN ROLLAND, 19th-/20th-century French writer

Are we not one? Are we not joined by heaven? Each interwo-ven\ with the other's fate?

–HANDWRITTEN VERSE on an 1852 Valentine's Day card

What greater thing is there for two human souls than to feel that they are joined . . . to strengthen each other . . . to be at one with each other in silent unspeakable memories.

–GEORGE ELIOT, 19th-century English novelist

Vows And Blessings

To have and to hold from this day forward, for better for worse, for richer for poorer, in sickness, and in health, to love and to cherish, till death do us part, according to God's holy ordinance.

–FROM *The Book of Common Prayer*

And God blessed them, and God said unto them, Be fruitful, and multiply, and replenish the earth, and subdue it.

–GENESIS 1:28, *The Holy Bible,* King James version

May fortune bless you! May the middle distance
Of your young life be pleasant as the foreground—
The joyous foreground! And, when you have reached it,
May that which now is the far-off horizon
(But which will then become the middle distance),
In fruitful promise be exceeded only
By that which will have opened, in the meantime,
Into a new and glorious horizon!

–DR. DALY, in *The Sorcerer,* written by Sir William Gilbert (librettist) and
Sir Arthur Sullivan (lyricist)

Be thou magnified, O bridegroom, like Abraham, and blessed like Isaac, and increase like Jacob, walking in peace and living in righteousness . . .

–FROM GREEK ORTHODOX MARRIAGE SERVICE

[T]hou, O bride, be magnified like Sarah, and rejoice like Rebecca, and increase like Rachel, being glad in thy husband and keeping the bounds of the law . . .

—FROM GREEK ORTHODOX MARRIAGE SERVICE

Open the temple gate unto my love,
Open them wide that she may enter in . . .

—EDMUND SPENSER, 16th-century English poet, from "Epithalamion"

In the words of the English service, "Listen all ye that are present; those that were distant are now brought together; those that were separated are now united.

—ERNEST CRAWLEY, social anthropologist and writer, from *The Mystic Rose: A Study of Primitive Marriage and of Primitive Thought in Its Bearing on Marriage*

Bring her up to the high altar, that she may
The Sacred ceremonies there partake,
The which do endless matrimony make . . .

—EDMUND SPENSER, 16th-century English poet, from "Epithalamion"

May the nights be honey-sweet for us; may the mornings be honey-sweet for us; may the earth be honey-sweet for us; may the heavens be honey-sweet for us . . . May the plants be honey-sweet for us; may the sun be all honey for us; may the cows yield honey-sweet milk!

—FROM THE HINDU MARRIAGE RITUAL OF "SEVEN STEPS"

In thine honor, my bridegroom, prosper and live;
    Let thy beauty arise and shine forth fierce;
    And the heart of thine enemies God shall pierce

And the sins of the thy youth will He forgive,
    And bless thee in increase and all thou shalt do.
    When thou settest thine hand thereto . . .

    –JUDAH HALEVI, 11th-/12th-century Spanish poet, philosopher, rabbi,
    from a poem to the bridegroom

Eternal God, creator and preserver of all life, author of salvation, and giver of all grace: Look with favor upon the world you have made, and for which your Son gave his life, and especially upon this man and this woman whom you make one flesh in Holy Matrimony.

Give them wisdom and devotion in the ordering of their common life, that each may be to the other a strength in need, a counselor in perplexity, a comfort in sorrow, and a companion in joy.

Grant that their wills may be so knit together in your will, and their spirit in your Spirit, that they may grow in love and peace with you and one another all the days of their life.

Give them grace, when they hurt each other, to recognize and acknowledge their fault, and to seek each other's forgiveness and yours.

Make their life together a sign of Christ's love to this sinful and broken world, that unity may overcome estrangement, forgiveness heal guilt, and joy conquer despair.

Bestow on them, if it is your will, the gift and heritage of children, and the grace to bring them up to know you, to love you, and to serve you.

Give them such fulfillment of their mutual affection that they may reach out in love and concern for others.

Grant that all married persons who have witnessed these vows find their lives strengthened and their loyalties confirmed.

Grant that the bonds of our common humanity, by which all

your children are united to one another, and the living to the
dead, may be so transformed by your grace, that your will may
be done on earth as it is in heaven; where, O Father, with your
Son and the Holy Spirit, you live and reign in perfect unity, now
and for ever.

–FROM *THE BOOK OF COMMON PRAYER*

A Prayer
For a Wedding
because everyone knows exactly what's good for another
because very few see
because a man and a woman may just possibly look at each
     other
because in the insanity of human relationships there still
     may come a time we say: yes, yes
because a man or a woman can do anything he or she
     pleases.
because you can reach any point in your life saying: now, I
     want this
because eventually it occurs we want each other, we want
     to know each other, even stupidly, even uglily
because there is at best a simple need in two people to try
     and reach some simple ground
because that simple ground is not so simple
because we are human beings gathered together whether
     we like it or not
because we are human beings reaching out to touch
because sometimes we grow
     we ask a blessing on this marriage
     we ask that some simplicity be allowed
     we ask their happiness

we ask that this couple be known for what it is,
and that the light shine upon it
we ask a blessing for their marriage.

–JOEL OPPENHEIMER, 20th-century American poet and columnist, "A
Prayer for a Wedding"

. . . I bring
To thee this ring,
Made for thy finger fit;
To show by this
That our love is
Or should be, like it.

–ROBERT HERRICK, 17th-century English poet, from "To Julia"

If you, X, take this woman, Y,
and if you, Y, take this man, X,
you two who have taken each other
many times before, then this
is something to be trusted . . .

–STEPHEN DUNN, contemporary American poet, from "Epithalamion"

In the words of the English service, "For this cause shall a man
leave his father and mother and shall be unto his wife; and they
two shall be one flesh."

–ERNEST CRAWLEY, social anthropologist and writer, from *The Mystic Rose:
A Study of Primitive Marriage and of Primitive Thought in Its Bearing on Marriage*

Now again, our Master, we beseech thee, may thy servants be
worthy of the mark of the sign of thy Word through the bond of

betrothal, their love for one another inviolable through the firm sureness of their union.

—From the Coptic Orthodox marriage service

Blessed are you, Holy One of the Earth, who creates the fruit of the vine.
Blessed are you, Holy One of the Universe. You created all things for your Glory.
Blessed are you, Holy One of the World. Through you mankind lives.
Blessed are you, Holy One of the World. You made man and woman in your image, after your likeness, that they might perpetuate life . . .
Blessed are you, Holy One of All Nature, who makes Zion rejoice with her children . . .
Blessed are you, Holy One of the Cosmos, who makes the bridegroom and bride rejoice.
Blessed are you, Holy One of All, who created joy and gladness; bride and bridegroom, mirth and song, pleasure and delight, love, fellowship, peace and friendship . . .

—The Hebrew "Seven Blessings"

Blessed be You, Life-Spirit of the universe,
Who makes a distinction between holy and not yet holy,
between light and darkness,
between Shabbat and the six days of the week,
between committed and uncommitted,
between common goals and personal goals,
between love and aloneness.
Blessed be you,
Who distinguished between what is holy, and what is not yet holy.

—Hebrew blessing for the Sabbath end

This is a wedding of two people, not two roles. Karin and Martin are here—not A Bride, not A Groom. Not one person and one possession. No one but no one—not even her family, not even we who are her sisters—can give Karin away. And no one can be given her. She belongs to herself.

>   –A WEDDING ATTENDED BY FEMINIST GLORIA STEINEM included this passage
>   in the ceremony

Thy bosom is endeared with all hearts,
Which I by lacking have supposed dead;
And there reigns love and all love's loving parts,
And all those friends which I thought buried.
How many a holy and obsequious tear
Hath dear religious love stolen from mine eye,
As interest of the dead, which now appear,
But things remov'd that hidden in there lie.
Thou art the grave where buried love doth live.
Hung with the trophies of my lovers gone
Who all their parts of me to thee did give;
That due of many now is thine alone.
God, the best maker of all marriages,
Combine yours hearts in one.

>   –WILLIAM SHAKESPEARE, 16th-/17th-century English poet and playwright,
>   Sonnet XXXI

You will reciprocally promise love,
loyalty and matrimonial honesty.
We only want for you this day
that these words constitute
the principle of your entire life;
and that with the help
of the divine grace
you will observe these solemn vows

that today, before God,
you formulate.

—Pope John Paul II

Virgins call on you to prepare them for marriage and
The bride calls on you to make sure
Her husband's manhood will stand shining forever.
Hail, O sacred father Priapus, hail!

—Prayer to Priapus, ancient Greek god of fertility

The union of husband and wife in heart, body, and mind is in-
tended by God for their mutual joy; for the help and comfort
given one another in prosperity and adversity; and, when it is
God's will, for the procreation of children and their nurture in
the knowledge and love of the Lord.

—From "The Celebration and Blessing of a Marriage" in *The Book of
Common Prayer*

At its most basic, believing and celebrating the contract you are
entering upon means there is at least a chance that both partners
have some optimism and commitment; at its most abstract such
a ceremony has the capacity to define and possibly sustain a
marriage.

—Rosie Scott, contemporary Australian writer

If I had this day to live over, I wouldn't change one blessed thing.
Not one step that got me here with you, right now. I want to be
here. I belong here. I love you more than anything. And what's
more . . . I don't want to live without you. You are an answer to

a very big question: Where's the rest of my heart? . . . You're in my blood. You're in a place in me so deep no one else is ever gonna be able to get there again.

–TAD MARTIN (ACTOR MICHAEL E. KNIGHT), to his bride DIXIE COONEY
(ACTRESS CADY MCCLAIN) on the daytime drama *All My Children,* 1989

For all that has been—thanks!
To all that shall be—yes!

–DAG HAMMARSKJÖLD, former Secretary General of the United Nations

Wedding Day

I would like to say a few words about weddings. I've just been through one. Not my own. My daughter's . . . I always used to think that marriage was a simple affair. Boy and girl meet. They fall in love, get married. They have babies. Eventually the babies grow up and meet other babies. They fall in love and get married and so on and on and on. It's not only simple, it's downright monotonous. But I was wrong. I figured without the wedding.

–STANLEY BANKS (ACTOR SPENCER TRACY), in the movie *Father of the Bride,* 1950

A wedding, a church wedding, it's what every girl dreams of. A bridal dress, orange blossoms, the music. It's something lovely for her to remember all her life. And something for us to remember, too.

–ELLIE BANKS (ACTRESS JOAN BENNETT), in the movie *Father of the Bride,* 1950

[There was a seriousness to it, but] we [also] saw it as a chance to throw a really big party.

> –SCOTT IAN, guitarist for the heavy metal band Anthrax, commenting on his wedding to Debbie Leavitt

On behalf of everyone here, let me just say, "Wow!"

> –PASTOR MARK PICKERILL, presiding over the real-life wedding of TV hero *Hercules*, actor Kevin Sorbo, and actress Sam Jenkins

At all times: Always remember that this is your day and that you should have it run as you want it. Keep in mind that it is the most romantic and wonderful day in your life.

> –"YOUR WEDDING," as appeared in a 1993 Australian newspaper article

To church in the morning, and there saw a wedding in the church, which I have not seen in many a day; and the young people so merry one with another! And strange to see what delight we married people have to see these poor fools decoyed into our condition, every man and woman gazing and smiling at them.

> –SAMUEL PEPYS, from his diary, December 28, 1665

The relationship between the meaningfulness and beauty of a ceremony and the ensuing success of the marriage is not exactly the stuff of mathematical certainty, but the redefinition of the whole idea of marriage, that is, equality, mutual respect, and flexibility of roles, has to start somewhere in a way that is significant to both partners.

> –ROSIE SCOTT, contemporary Australian writer

Dear bride, remember, if you can,
That thing you married is a man.

His thoughts are low, his mind is earthy,
Of you he is totally unworthy;
Wherein lies a lesson too few have learnt it—
That's the reason you married him, aren't it?

The organ booms, the procession begins,
The rejected suitors square their chins,
And angels swell the harmonious tide
Of blessings upon the bonnie bride.
But blessings also on him without whom
There would be no bride. I mean the groom.

> —Ogden Nash, 20th-century American poet, from "Everybody Loves a Bride, Even the Groom"

Your wedding really starts long before the event takes place. It begins the moment you find yourself thinking, This is the man I want to marry—I wonder if he feels the same about me?

> —Emily Post, etiquette maven, from *Complete Book of Wedding Etiquette,* 1982

Your wedding should be like naming your child. Make sure it is what you really want. Make it your fantasy—not your mother's or your sister's or your friend's. That's what I did, and I had a great time!

> —Maggie Delgado, costume designer for the daytime TV drama, *All My Children*

Tonight is a night of union and also of scattering of the stars, for a bride is coming from the sky; the full moon.
The sky is an astrolabe, and the Law is Love.

> —Jalāl al-Dīn Rūmī, 13th-century Persian poet

The little house was not far away, and the only bridal journey Meg had was the quiet walk with John, from the old home to the new. When she came down, looking like a pretty Quakeress in her dove-colored suit and straw bonnet tied with white, they all gathered about her to say "good-bye," as tenderly as if she had been going to make the grand tour . . .

They stood watching her, with faces full of love and hope and tender pride, as she walked away, leaning on her husband's arm, with her hands full of flowers, and the June sunshine brightening her happy face,—and so Meg's married life began.

–LOUISA MAY ALCOTT, 19th-century American writer, from her novel,
  Little Women

Now join your hands, and with your hands your hearts.

–WILLIAM SHAKESPEARE, 16th-/17th-century English poet and playwright,
  from *King Henry VI*

Whatever size or style of wedding you choose, it is the careful, thoughtful planning and the atmosphere—not the cost—that makes it beautiful. It is not how much you spend but how you spend that matters.

–EMILY POST, etiquette maven, from *Complete Book of Wedding Etiquette*,
  1982

I have always known
That at last I would
Take this road, but yesterday
I did not know that it would be today.

–KENNETH REXROTH, 20th-century American poet, from *One Hundred
  Poems from the Japanese*

The bride had begged her father to be spared the usual marriage pleasantries. However, a fishmonger, one of their cousins (who had even brought a pair of soles for his wedding present), began to squirt water from his mouth through the keyhole, when old Rouault came up just in time to stop him, and explain to him that the distinguished position of his son-in-law would not allow of such liberties . . .

–GUSTAVE FLAUBERT, 19th-century French writer, from *Madame Bovary*

On the night of the wedding ceremony, the rapt attention focused upon me, especially by my friends, increased my joy so that I almost leaped with delight while I donned my wedding dress embroidered in threads of silver and gold. I was spellbound by the diamonds and other brilliant jewels that crowned my head and sparkled on my bodice and arms. All of this dazzled me and kept me from thinking of anything else. I was certain I would remain forever in this raiment, the centre of attention and admiration . . . He led me by the hand to the bridal throne and took his place beside me. All the while, I was trembling like a branch in a storm. The groom addressed a few words to me but I understood nothing . . . Finally my new husband took me by the hand. In my daze I knew not where I was being led.

–HUDA SHAARAWI, from *Harem Years: Memories of an Egyptian Feminist*

Let all thy joys be as the month of May,
And all thy days be as a marriage day.

–FRANCIS QUARLES, 16th-/17th-century English poet, from "To a Bride"

The wind blew all my wedding day,
And my wedding-night was the night of the high wind;
And a stable door was banging, again and again,
That he must go and shut it, leaving me.

I was sad
That any man or beast that night should lack
The happiness I had.

> –Philip Larkin, 20th-century British poet, novelist and critic, from "Wedding Wind"

Therefore must the bride below have a canopy, all beautiful with decorations prepared for her, in order to honor the Bride above, who comes to be present and participate in the joy of the bride below. For this reason it is necessary that the canopy be as beautiful as possible, and that the Supernal Bride be invited to come and share in the joy.

> –From "Teremah," from the Zohar, 13th-century seminal work of Jewish mysticism

Come along! Today is a festival!
Clap your hands and say, "The is a day of happiness!"
Who in the world is like this bridal pair?
The earth and the sky are full of sugar. Sugar cane is sprouting
    all around!
We can hear the roar of the pearly ocean. The whole world is
    full of waves!
The voices of Love are approaching from all sides. We are
    On our way to heaven!
Once upon a time we played with angels. Let's all go back up
    there again.

Heaven is our home! Yes, we are even higher up than heaven,
    Higher than the angels!
My dear, it's true that spiritual beauty is wonderful. But your
loveliness in this world is even more so!

> –JALĀL AL-DĪN RŪMĪ, 13th-century Persian poet, adapted from the transla-
> tion by A. J. Arberry

. . . may her bridegroom bring her to a house
Where all's accustomed, ceremonious;
For arrogance and hatred are the wares
Peddled in the thoroughfares.
How but in custom and in ceremony
Are innocence and beauty born?
Ceremony's a name for the rich horn,
And custom for the spreading laurel tree.

> –WILLIAM BUTLER YEATS, 19th-/20th-century Irish poet and dramatist,
> from "A Prayer for My Daughter"

After his wedding, the author Arthur Kober sent the following
telegram to the regular players at his weekly poker club: "Sorry I
can't join you tonight as there is no way of bettering the perfect
hand I am now holding."

> –ANONYMOUS

The bride . . . floating all white beside her father in the morning
shadow of trees, her veil flowing with laughter.

> –D. H. LAWRENCE, 19th-/20th-century English writer

A happy bridesmaid makes a happy bride.

> –LORD ALFRED TENNYSON, 19th-century English poet

Next to the bride and groom themselves, the best man is the most important member of the wedding.

—EMILY POST, etiquette maven, from *Complete Book of Wedding Etiquette,* 1982

She stood in the corner of the bride's room, wanting to say: I love the two of you so much and you are the we of me. Please take me with you from the wedding, for we belong together . . . her tongue was heavy in her mouth and dumb. She could only speak in a voice that shook a little—to ask where was the veil?

—CARSON MCCULLERS, 20th-century American novelist and playwright, from *The Member of the Wedding*

The wedding is the chief ceremony of the middle-class mythology (of love and marriage), and it functions as the official entrée of the spouses to their middle-class status. This is the real meaning of saving up to get married.

—GERMAINE GREER, contemporary Australian feminist writer

Wives

Of all the home remedies, a good wife is the best.

—KIN HUBBARD, 19th-/20th-century American journalist and humorist

An ideal wife is one who remains faithful to you but tries to be just as charming as if she weren't.

—SACHA GUITRY, 19th-/20th-century French actor, playwright and director

An ideal wife is any woman who has an ideal husband.

—BOOTH TARKINGTON, 19th-/20th-century American novelist

Harpo, she's a lovely person, She deserves a good husband. Marry her before she finds one.

—OSCAR LEVANT, 20th-century composer, musician, actor, to Harpo Marx upon meeting Harpo's fiancée

Stella: Every man's ready for marriage when the right girl comes along . . .

Jeff: She's not the right girl for me.

Stella: Yeah she's perfect.

Jeff: If she was only ordinary.

Stella: Yep I can hear you now. Get out of my life you perfectly wonderful woman, you're too good for me.

—STELLA (ACTRESS THELMA RITTER) to JEFF (ACTOR JAMES STEWART) in the movie *Rear Window*

I have come to the conclusion never again to think of marrying, and for this reason, I can never be satisfied with anyone who would be blockhead enough to have me.

—ABRAHAM LINCOLN, in a letter to Mrs. O. H. Browning, April 1, 1838

No matter how happily a woman may be married, it always pleases her to discover that there is a nice man who wishes she were not.

—H. L. MENCKEN, 20th-century American writer

No happiness is like unto it, no love so great as that of man and wife, no such comfort as a sweet wife.

—ROBERT BURTON, 16th-/17th-century English author and clergyman

The world well tried—the sweetest thing in life
Is the unclouded welcome of a wife.

> –N. P. WILLIS, 19th-century American poet and writer

A wife is one who shares her husband's thoughts, incorporates his heart in love with hers, and crowns him with her trust. She is God's remedy for loneliness and God's reward for all the toil of life.

> –HENRY VAN DYKE, 19th-/20th-century writer

If it hadn't been for my wife, I couldn't have stood married life.

> –DON HEROLD, writer

I want (who does not want?) a wife,
    Affectionate and fair,
To solace all the woes of life,
    And all its joys to share;
Of temper sweet, of yielding will,
    Of firm, yet placid mind,
With all my faults to love me still,
    With sentiment refin'd.

> –JOHN QUINCY ADAMS, 6th U.S. president

She is a winsome wee thing,
She is a handsome wee thing,
She is a lo'esome wee thing,
This sweet wee wife o' mine.

> –ROBERT BURNS, 18th-century Scottish poet, from "My Wife's a Winsome Wee Thing"

I need a hand to nail the right,
A help, a love, a you, a wife.

> –ALAN DUGAN, contemporary American poet, from "Love Song: I and Thou"

An intelligent wife sees through a husband, an understanding wife sees him through.

> –ANONYMOUS

A good wife is like the ivy which beautifies the building to which it clings, twining tendrils more lovingly as time converts the ancient edifice into ruins.

> –SAMUEL JOHNSON, 18th-century English dictionary inventor/lexicographer

I should like to know what is the proper function of women, if it is not to make reasons for husbands to stay home, and still stronger reasons for bachelors to go out.

> –GEORGE ELIOT, 19th-century English novelist

Husbands, love your wives.

> –EPHESIANS 5:25, *The Holy Bible,* King James version

A man's best possession is a sympathic wife.

> –EURIPIDES, ancient Greek dramatist

All men, except the most brutish, desire to have, in the woman most nearly connected with them, not a forced slave but a willing one, not a slave merely, but a favourite.

> –JOHN STUART MILL, 19th-century English philosopher and economist

Live joyfully with the wife whom thou lovest all the days of the life of thy vanity, which he hath given thee under the sun, all the days of thy vanity: for that is thy portion in this life, and in thy labour which thou takest under the sun.

–ECCLESIASTES 9:9, *The Holy Bible,* King James version

Every married man should believe there's but one good wife in the world, and that's his own.

–JONATHAN SWIFT, 17th-/18th-century English author and satirist

I chose my wife, as she did her wedding gown, not for a fine glossy surface, but such qualities as would wear well.

–OLIVER GOLDSMITH, 18th-century Anglo-Irish playwright, novelist and poet, from *The Victor of Wakefield*

How much the wife is dearer than the bride.

–LORD LYTTLETON, 18th-century English poet

You are my true and honorable wife,
Dear as the ruddy drops that warm my heart.

–THOMAS GRAY, 18th-century English poet

All the molestations of marriage are abundantly recompensed with the comforts which God bestoweth on them who make a wise choice of a wife.

–THOMAS FULLER, 17th-century English author

If you have the good luck to find a modest wife, you should prostrate yourself before the Tarpeian threshold, and sacrifice a heifer with gilded horns to Juno.

–JUVENAL, 1st-century Roman poet

You have been such light to me that other women have been your shadows.

> –WENDELL BERRY, contemporary poet and essayist, from "The Country of Marriage"

In my Sunday school class there was a beautiful little girl with golden curls. I was smitten with her once and still am.

> –HARRY S. TRUMAN, 33rd U.S. president

A wife is essential to great longevity; she is the receptacle of half a man's cares, and two-thirds of his ill-humor.

> –CHARLES READE, 19th-century English dramatist

A man loved by a beautiful and virtuous woman carries with him a talisman that renders him invulnerable; every one feels that such a one's life has a higher value than that of others.

> –MADAME AMANDINE AURORE LUCIE DUDEVANT (A.K.A. GEORGE SAND), 19th-century French novelist

To the wife of my bosom
All happiness from everything
And her husband
May he be good and considerate
Gay and cheerful and restful.
And make her the best wife
In the world . . .

> –GERTRUDE STEIN, 20th-century American writer, from *Patriarchal Poetry*

Child to mother, sheep to fold
Bird to nest from wandering wide:
Happy bridegroom, seek your bride.

> –A. E. HOUSMAN, 19th-/20th-century English poet and scholar, from "Epithalamium"

Being a wife is one of the few occupations where experience on the job doesn't increase your value or lead to a better offer the second time around.

–LYNNE SPENDER, contemporary Australian feminist author

Married life is a woman's profession; and to this life, her training—that of dependence—is modeled.

–FROM THE *BRITISH SATURDAY REVIEW,* 1857

. . . said Susanna . . . "I'd have another wedding—but next time round I'd make sure I married someone who didn't want a wife."

–ANONYMOUS, from the book *Weddings and Wives* by Dale Spender

It's true that I did get the girl, but then my grandfather always said, "Even a blind chicken finds a few grains of corn now and then."

–LYLE LOVETT, contemporary musician, upon marrying actress Julia Roberts, 1994 (They have since divorced.)

Man gets nothing brighter than a kind wife . . .

–SEMONIDES, Greek poet of the 7th-century, B.C.

Words About Husbands

One good husband is worth two good wives; for the scarcer things are, the more they're valued.

–BENJAMIN FRANKLIN, 18th-century American patriot, diplomat, author, printer, scientist and inventor, from *Poor Richard's Almanac,* 1733

Husbands are things wives have to get used to putting up with, And with whom they breakfast with and sup with.

They interfere with the disciplines of nurseries,
And forget anniversaries,
And when they have been particularly remiss
They think they can cure everything with a great big kiss.

–OGDEN NASH, 20th-century American poet

[For a woman] a ship captain is a good man to marry . . . for absences are a good influence in love . . . It is to be noticed that those who have loved once or twice already are so much the better educated to a woman's hand . . . Lastly, no woman should marry a teetotaller, or a man who does not smoke.

–ROBERT LOUIS STEVENSON, 19th-century Scottish novelist, from *Virginibus Puerisque*

My husband will never chase another woman. He's too fine, too decent, too old.

–COMEDIAN GRACIE ALLEN, wife of comedian George Burns

Errol Flynn died on a 70-foot boat with a 17-year-old girl. Walter has always wanted to go that way, but he's going to settle for a 17-footer with a 70-year-old.

–BETSY CRONKITE, wife of newsman Walter Cronkite

I've been married to one Marxist and one Fascist, and neither one would take the garbage out.

–LEE GRANT, American actress

Sexiness wears thin after a while and beauty fades, but to be married to a man who makes you laugh every day, ah, now that's a real treat!

–JOANNE WOODWARD, American actress married to actor Paul Newman

Husband, destiny, my Unknown, You are the spirit who calls
    me.
Your ring burns fire on my flesh, Willingly I am marked by you.

> –FROM THE OPERA *BRIDE OF FORTUNE* by Anna Maria Dell'oso and Gillian
> Whitehead

An archaeologist is the best husband a woman can have; the
older she gets, the more interested he is in her.

> –AGATHA CHRISTIE, British mystery writer

Ah Mozart! He was happily married—but his wife wasn't.

> –VICTOR BORGE, contemporary Danish musician and comedian

Apparently I am going to marry Charles Lindbergh . . . Don't
wish me happiness—it's gotten beyond that, somehow. Wish
me courage and strength and a sense of humor—I will need
them all . . .

> –ANNE MORROW LINDBERGH, 20th-century American writer and the wife
> of aviator Charles Lindbergh, from *Bring Me a Unicorn*

Perfection is what American women expect to find in their husbands . . . but English women only hope to find in their butlers.

> –W. SOMERSET MAUGHAM, 20th-century English writer

I think men who have a pieced ear are better prepared for marriage. They've experienced pain and bought jewelry.

> –RITA RUDNER, contemporary American comedian

Some of us are becoming the men we wanted to marry.

> –GLORIA STEINEM, 20th-century American feminist

It takes a man twenty-five years to learn to be married; it's a wonder women have the patience to wait for it.

–CLARENCE B. KELLAND, 20th-century American author

Enjoy your husband, but never think you know him thoroughly.

–LADYBIRD JOHNSON, wife of 36th U.S. president, Lyndon B. Johnson

Chapter 2

For Better or for Worse

Compromise / Tolerance . . . and Lack Thereof

To keep your marriage brimming, with love in the wedding cup, whenever you're wrong, admit it; whenever you're right, shut up.

–OGDEN NASH, 20th-century American poet

Only two things are necessary to keep one's wife happy. One is to let her think she is having her own way, and the other, to let her have it.

–LYNDON B. JOHNSON, 36th U.S. president

"You mean in all the years you've always had the last words when you argue with Lily?"
    "Yes, and they're always the same ones—'You're right.'"

–ANONYMOUS

Keep your eyes wide open before marriage, and half shut afterwards.

> –BENJAMIN FRANKLIN, 18th-century American patriot, diplomat, author, printer, scientist and inventor, from *Poor Richard's Almanac*, 1733

Maybe it is our imperfections which make us so perfect for one another.

> –The utterly perfect MR. KNIGHTLY (JEREMY NORTHAM) to the equally flawless Emma (GWYNETH PALTROW) in the movie *Emma*, based on the novel of the same name by Jane Austen

Two persons who have chosen each other out of all the species, with the design to be each other's mutual comfort and entertainment, have, in that action, bound themselves to be good-humored, affable, discreet, forgiving, patient, and joyful, with respect to each other's frailties and imperfections, to the end of their lives.

> –JOSEPH ADDISON, 17th-/18th-century English essayist and poet

I love this little lady. Some of you still can't believe that. You're too busy pointing out her faults. Well, guess what? I've heard rumors I may have one or two myself.

> –ASA BUCHANAN (ACTOR PHILIP CAREY), saying his vows to his TV bride, Alex Olanov, (ACTRESS TONJA WALKER) on the daytime drama *One Life to Live*, 1994

With all thy faults, I love thee still.

> –WILLIAM COWPER, 18th-century English poet

I'll give you the future if you'll forgive me my past.

> –KENNY ROGERS, country music star, to his bride, Wanda Miller, after they exchanged vows

Marrying a man is like buying something you've been admiring for a long time in a shop window. You may love it when you get it home, but it doesn't always go with everything in the house.

—JEAN KERR, 20th-century American humorist

The kindest and the happiest pair will find occasion to forbear; and something, every day they live, to pity and perhaps forgive.

—WILLIAM COWPER, 18th-century English poet

Marriage is three parts love
And seven parts forgiveness

—LANGDON MITCHELL, 19th-/20th-century playwright

Sometimes you have to look hard at a person and remember that he's doing the best he can. He's just trying to find his way, that's all . . . just like you.

—ETHEL THAYER (ACTRESS KATHARINE HEPBURN), in the movie *On Golden Pond*

To say the words "love and compassion" is easy. But to accept that love and compassion are built upon patience and perseverance is not easy. Your marriage will be firm and lasting if you remember this.

—BUDDHIST MARRIAGE HOMILY

To repress a harsh answer,
to confess a fault,
and to stop (right or wrong)
in the midst of self-defense,
in gentle submission,
sometimes requires
a struggle like life and death;
but these three efforts

are the golden threads with which
domestic happiness is woven.

—CAROLINE GILMAN, 19th-century American writer

Put on therefore, as the elect of God, holy and beloved, bowels
of mercies, kindness, humbleness of mind, meekness, long-
suffering;
Forbearing one another, and forgiving one another, if any man have
a quarrel against any: even as Christ forgave you, so also do ye.
And above all these things put on charity, which is the bond of
perfectness.
And let the peace of God rule in your hearts, to the which also
ye are called in one body; and be ye thankful.

—COLOSSIANS 3:12–15, *The Holy Bible,* King James version

Laugh and the world laughs with you. Snore and you sleep
alone.

—ANTHONY BURGESS, contemporary English writer

As a great part of the uneasiness of matrimony arises from mere
trifles, it would be wise in every young married man to enter
into an agreement with his wife that in all disputes the party
who was most convinced they were right would always surren-
der the victory. By this means both would be more forward to
give up the cause.

—HENRY FIELDING, 18th-century English novelist

Love has the patience
    to endure
The fault it sees
    But cannot cure.

—EDGAR GUEST, 20th-century American writer

Love is an act of endless forgiveness, a tender look which becomes a habit.

–PETER USTINOV, contemporary British actor and author

A wife has to thank God her husband has faults; a husband without faults is a dangerous observer.

–LORD HALIFAX, 17th-/18th-century English statesman and diplomat

You can never be happily married to one another until you get a divorce from yourself. Successful marriage demands a certain death to self.

–JERRY MCCANT, contemporary American author

The happiness of married life depends upon making small sacrifices with readiness and cheerfulness.

–JOHN SELDEN, 16th-/17th-century English jurist

It's really very simple. All you have to do is give up a little bit of you for him. Don't make everything a game, just late at night in that little room upstairs. Take care of him, make him feel important. If you can do that you'll have a happy and wonderful marriage.

–CORIE'S MOTHER (ACTRESS MILDRED NATWICK), to her daughter, Corie Bratter (ACTRESS JANE FONDA), in the movie *Barefoot in the Park*

Rendering good for ill,
Smiling at every frown,
Yielding your own self-will,
Laughing the tear-drops down:
Never a selfish whim,
Trouble, or pain to stir,
Everything for him,
Nothing at all for her!
Love that will aye endure,

Though the rewards be few,
That is the love that's pure,
That is the love that's true!

> –SIR WILLIAM GILBERT, 19th-/20th-century English dramatist, from *Patience or Bunthorne's Bride*

When you love someone you do not love them all the time, in exactly the same way, from moment to moment. It is an impossibility. It is even a lie to pretend to. And yet this is exactly what most of us demand. We have so little faith in the ebb and flow of life, of love, of relationships. We leap at the flow of the tide and resist in terror its ebb. We are afraid it will never return. We insist on permanency, on duration, on continuity; when the only continuity possible, in life as in love, is in growth, in fluidity—in freedom in the sense that the dancers are free, barely touching as they pass, but partners in the same pattern.

> –ANNE MORROW LINDBERGH, 20th-century American writer and the wife of aviator Charles Lindbergh, from *Gift from the Sea*

At his tenth anniversary, a man was asked if he and his wife ever had any differences of opinion.

"Many, many!" he nodded. "And important ones!"

"Then how come," asked his friend, "you seem to get along so well?"

"I never tell her about them."

> –ANONYMOUS

The reason that husbands and wives do not understand each other is because they belong to different sexes.

> –DOROTHY DIX, 20th-century American journalist

Marriage is a status of antagonistic cooperation. In such a status, necessarily, centripetal and centrifugal forces are continuously at work, and the measure of its success obviously depends on the extent to which the centripetal forces are predominant.

–JOHN M. WOOLSEY, federal judge

Constancy . . .

The motto of chivalry is also the motto of wisdom: to serve all, but love only one.

–HONORÉ DE BALZAC, 19th-century French novelist

O Firm one, pillar of the stars, Polestar, how stable you are! As the earth is stable, as the mountains are stable, as the universe is stable, so may this woman my wife be firm and stable in our family.

–Blessing recited by a Hindu groom, who represents Lord Shiva, creator and destroyer of the world, to his bride, who represents Lord Shiva's wife, Parvati, at the end of their wedding day

But if you please to do the duty of a true and loyal mistress and to give yourself heart and person to me, who will be as I have been, your most loyal servant (if your rigor does not forbid me) I promise you that not only the name shall be given you but also that I will take you for my mistress, cutting off all others that are in competition with you, out of my thoughts and affections, and serving you only.

–HENRY VIII, King of England to his second wife, Anne Boleyn (whom he later had beheaded)

Of all my loves the last, for here after I shall glow with passion for no other woman.

–HORACE, 1st-century, B.C., Roman poet and satirist

Buying a car, son, is just like getting married or going to New York City. Everybody ought to do it once, but nobody ought to do it twice.

> –OLD MAN HARRIS (ACTOR GEORGE FISHER) in the movie, *The Giant Gila Monster*

A prominent man, when asked what other person he would rather be than himself, replied, "My wife's second husband." That was true love and beautiful loyalty.

> –NATHAN H. GIST

If I had to live my life over again, I don't think I'd change it in any particular of the slightest consequence. I'd choose the same parents, the same birthplace, the same wife.

> –H. L. MENCKEN, 20th-century American satirist and essayist

If 20 years were to be erased and I were to be presented with the same choice again under the same circumstances I would act precisely as I did then . . . Perhaps I needed her even more in those searing lonely moments when I—I alone knew in my heart what my decision must be. I have needed her all these 20 years. I love her and need her now. I always will.

> –DUKE OF WINDSOR, on the 20th anniversary of his marriage to Wallis Warfield Simpson, for whom he abdicated as Edward VIII of England

The sum which two married people owe to one another defies calculation. It is an infinite debt, which can only be discharged through all eternity.

> –JOHANN WOLFGANG VON GOETHE, 18th-/19th-century German poet and dramatist, from *Effective Affinities*

Let every husband stay a lover true,
And every wife remain a sweetheart too.

—ANONYMOUS

Memo: not to adulterize my time by absenting myself from my
wife.

—SAMUEL TAYLOR COLERIDGE, 18th-/19th-century English poet

I have not spent a day without loving you; I have not spent a
night without embracing you . . . In the midst of my duties,
whether I am at the head of my army or inspecting the camps,
my beloved Josephine stands alone in my heart, occupies my
mind, fills my thoughts.

—NAPOLEON, 19th-century French emperor to his wife, Josephine

. . . on this spot—I believe on this very spot—I asked the permission of your mother two years ago to express to you my
love. She thought me a boy, and treated me as a boy. She said I
knew nothing of the world, and both our characters were un-
formed. I know the world now. I have committed many mistakes, doubtless many follies—have formed many opinions, and
have changed many opinions; but to one I have been constant, in
one I am unchanged—and that is my adoring love to you.

—BENJAMIN DISRAELI, 19th-century author and British prime minister, from
his novel *Lothair*

In the consciousness
of belonging together,
in the sense of constancy,
resides the sanctity,
the beauty of matrimony,
which helps us

to endure pain more easily,
to enjoy happiness doubly,
and to give rise to
the fullest and finest development
of our nature.

        –FANNY LEWALD, 19th-century German author

Let me not to marriage of true minds—
Admit impediments. Love is not love
Which alters when it alteration finds,
Or bends with the remover to remove:
O, no! it is an ever-fixed mark,
That looks on tempests and is never shaken;
Whose worth's unknown, although his height be taken.
Love's not Time's fool, though rosy lips and cheeks
Within his bending sickle's compass come;
Love alters not with his briefs hours and weeks,
But bears it out even to the edge of doom
    If this error, and upon me prov'd,
    I never writ, nor no man ever lov'd.

        –WILLIAM SHAKESPEARE, 16th-/17th-century English poet and playwright,
        Sonnet XXIII

Change everything, except your loves.

        –VOLTAIRE, 18th-century French writer and philosopher, from *Sur l'Usage*
        de la Vie

Now that I have taught you some respect for business and the
law, let me assure you that marriage is more sacred than either,
and that unless you are prepared to treat my wife with absolute
loyalty, you will be hurled into outer darkness for ever.
    The privilege of pawing me, such as it is, is hers exclusively.

She has to tolerate worshipping females whose efforts to conceal the fact that they take no interest in her are perfunctory, and who bore her to distraction with their adoration of me, but it is my business to see that her patience is not abused. Whenever I get anything in the nature of a love letter, I hand it straight to Charlotte.

–GEORGE BERNARD SHAW, 20th-century Irish-born British writer, to Erica Cotterill, in 1906, responding to her letter asking for his literary advice . . . and his love

. . . And Lack Thereof

. . . Affections, like the conscience, are rather to be led than drawn; and 'tis to be feared, that they marry where they do not love, will love where they do not marry.

–THOMAS FULLER, 17th-century English author

Where there is marriage without love, there will be love without marriage.

–BENJAMIN FRANKLIN, 18th-century American patriot, diplomat, author, printer, scientist and inventor

I say I don't sleep with married men. But what I meant is that I don't sleep with happily married men.

–BRITT EKLAND, contemporary Swedish actress

It is not marriage that fails; it is the people that fail. All that marriage does is to show people up.

–HARRY EMERSON FOSDICK 19th-/20th-century American clergyman

And the next time, Arthur, when you offer yourself to a woman, — do not say as you have done to me, "I have no heart—I do not love you; but I am ready to marry you because my mother wishes for the match." We require more than this in return for our love . . .

–W. M. THACKERY, 19th-century English writer, from *Pendennis*

Etiquette, Fashion and Beauty

My one rule is that I do not want a bride coming down the aisle seven months pregnant.

–JOAN RIVERS, comedian, commenting on her daughter Melissa's wedding

Chaperonage is not a girl's lot today, but there are still a few wise rules best to observe. Even an engaged couple may not spend the night under the same roof without the presence of someone to chaperone them . . . must never do anything or cause talk or lower his or her esteem in the public mind. Hackneyed but true. "Discretion is the better part of valor." Just being engaged doubles your visibility in the public eye.

–*The Bride's Book of Etiquette,* 1948

An engaged couple observes the same rules that are socially acceptable for any single man or woman. They do not stay overnight together under one roof unless some older person is also in the house. They may travel unchaperoned on the same ship, even though the trip is overnight—with separate baths. They would not be likely to travel in an automobile alone on an overnight trip. Good judgment and taste will guide them correctly.

> −*The Bride's School Complete Book of Engagement and Wedding Etiquette,*
> 1959

When an engaged couple must travel unaccompanied overnight on a public conveyance, their accommodations should not be adjoining, and the presence of a chaperon would be in order at the destination . . . Unmarried contemporaries are not considered suitable as chaperons, and an engaged pair traveling by automobile may not, with propriety, make overnight stops at hotels or motor inns, either by themselves or accompanied only by unmarried friends of the same age.

> −EMILY POST, etiquette maven, from *Etiquette,* 1969

It is far better to think how much they [the engaged couple] may be bursting with physical desire for each other than to see them actually demonstrating it.

> −AMY VANDERBILT, socialite and etiquette maven, from *Complete Book of Etiquette,* 1978

If your parents aren't acquainted with your fiancé yet, a letter or note asking them to please "invite someone very special" for a weekend or holiday works nicely. You needn't say anything until your fiancé feels comfortable and at home—rest assured, your parents will have a hint of your plans. (Incidentally, even if you are already sharing an apartment or house, you shouldn't expect to share a room in your parents' home if this makes them uneasy.)

> −*The New Bride's Book of Etiquette,* 1981

An engagement ring is not essential to becoming engaged.

> −EMILY POST, etiquette maven, from *Complete Book of Wedding Etiquette,*
> 1982

... the Law of Nature—she's got ten fingers so you've got to have rings for some of them and one of them is apparently for the engagement ring.

> —SIMON MAYO AND MARTIN WROE, contemporary British humorists and authors

For in what stupid age or nation
Was marriage ever out of fashion?

> —SAMUEL BUTLER, British author

I looked like Count Chocula.

> —MICHAEL LEWIS, author, husband of MTV News anchor Tabitha Soren, commenting on his wedding-day get-up for Soren's desired King Arthur–style affair.

A handsome man now looks handsome.
A good man will soon take on beauty.

> —SAPPHO, Greek poet of the 7th-century, B.C.

I'll let you in on a secret. The only women who even come close to wearing their wedding dress again are those who don't wear white. They're not in the last bit romantic, they're just good planners.

> —JAN OWEN, contemporary Australian author

Think about the image that you want to project and don't be pressured into accepting what someone else thinks you should be. Getting married is a very stressful experience—you don't want to wake up on the morning of your wedding saying, "What is this costume I'm wearing?" Your wedding dress should be a reflection of you—don't be afraid of expressing who you are.

–Susan Gammie, costume designer for the daytime TV drama, *One Life to Live*

I am under the distinct impression that there are more brides traipsing down the aisle in rented or unpaid-off mock virginal finery in 1993 that there have ever been before in the history of the world.

–Germaine Greer, contemporary Australian feminist writer

A woman seldom asks advice before she has bought her wedding clothes.

–Joseph Addison, 17th-/18th-century English essayist and poet

The most beautiful thing in the world is a match well made.

–Emma (actress Gwyneth Paltrow) at the marriage of her former governess, in the movie *Emma*, based on the novel of the same name by Jane Austen

There is something about a wedding-gown prettier than any other gown in the world.

–Douglas Jerrold, 19th-century English playwright and humorist

When in the chronicle of wasted time
I see descriptions of the fairest wights,
And beauty making beautiful old rhyme
In praise of ladies dead and lovely knights,

Then, in the blazon of sweet beauty's best,
Of hand, of foot, of lip, of eye, of brow,
I see their antique pen would have express'd
Even such a beauty as you master now.
So all their praises are but prophecies
Of this our time, all you prefiguring;
And, for they look'd but with divining eyes,
They had not skill enough your worth to sing;

For we, which now behold these present days,
Have eyes to wonder, but lack tongues to praise.

–WILLIAM SHAKESPEARE, 16th-/17th-century English poet and playwright,
Sonnet XIX

Behold, thou art fair, my love; behold, thou art fair; thou hast
doves' eyes within thy locks: thy hair is as a flock of goats,
that appear from Mount Gilead.
Thy teeth are like a flock of sheep that are even shorn, which
came up from the washing; whereof every one bear twins,
and none is barren among them.
Thy lips are like a threat of scarlet, and thy speech is comely:
thy temples are like a piece of a pomegranate within thy
locks.
Thy neck is like the tower of David builded for an armoury,
whereon there hang a thousand bucklers, all shields of
mighty men.
Thy two breasts are like two young roes that are twins, which
feed among the lilies.
Until the day break, and the shadows flee away, I will get me to
the mountain of myrrh, and to the hill of frankincense.
Thou art all fair, my love; there is no spot in thee.

–SONG OF SOLOMON 4:1–7, *The Holy Bible,* King James version

Thou are beautiful, O my love, as Tirzah, comely as Jerusalem, terrible as an army with banners.

Turn away thine eyes from me, for they have overcome me:

> —Song of Solomon 6:4–7, *The Holy Bible,* King James version

You've gotta get married before your hips start spreading and you get facial hair.

> —Wedding advice from Angie Sullivan (actress Christina Pickles) to Julia Sullivan (actress Drew Barrymore), in the movie *The Wedding Singer*

Fighting

. . . being married is different spiritually . . . [but] we're still yelling at each other.

> —Rosemary Clooney, singer, speaking at the reception of her wedding to Dante DiPaolo

A married couple are well suited when both partners usually feel the need for a quarrel at the same time.

> —Jean Rostand, 19th-/20th-century French essayist, satirist and biologist, known for revolutionizing the field of artificial insemination

We both said "I do" and we haven't agreed on a single thing since.

> —Stuart Mackenzie (actor Mike Myers), toasting his wife on their 30th wedding anniversary, in the movie *So I Married an Axe Murderer*

Almost all married people fight, although many are ashamed to admit it. Actually a marriage in which no quarreling at all takes place may well be one that is dead or dying from emotional under-nourishment. If you care, you probably fight.

–FLORA DAVIS, British author and composer

Whenever I hear people say they have lived together twenty-five years and never had the least difference I wonder whether they have not had a good deal of indifference.

–ROBERT COLLYER, 19th-/20th-century British-born American clergyman

Nagging is the repetition of unpalatable truths.

–BARONESS EDITH SUMMERSKILL, president of Britain's Married Women's Association in the 1950s

Most married couples, even though they love each other very much in theory, tend to view each other in practice as large teeming flaw colonies, the result being that they get on each other's nerves and regularly erupt into vicious emotional shouting matches over such issues as toaster settings.

–DAVE BARRY, contemporary American humorist

"What's your formula for a successful marriage," the husband was asked on his 32nd anniversary.
   "Never show your worst side to your better half."

–ANONYMOUS

"Communication," said the husband on his 10th anniversary, "is the key to a happy marriage. When I talk, she listens. When she talks, I listen. And when we both talk—the neighbors listen."

–ANONYMOUS

Hardship

The course of true love never did run smooth.

> –WILLIAM SHAKESPEARE, 16th-/17th-century English poet and playwright

When it is dark and there is trouble, you need but wave that bauble and there will be light.

> –WILLIAM SHATNER, a.k.a. television's Captain Kirk, speaking while plac-
> ing a diamond on his wife's hand.

. . . Many waters cannot quench love, neither can the floods drown it . . .

> –SONG OF SOLOMON 8:7, *The Holy Bible,* King James version

I'll love him more, more
Than e'er wife loved before,
Be the days dark or bright.

> –JEAN INGELOW, 19th-century English writer, from the poem "Seven
> Times Three"

Trouble is part of your life, and if you don't share it, you don't give the person that loves you enough chance to love you enough.

> –DINAH SHORE, 20th-century American singer/actress

With thee all toils are sweet; each clime hath charms; earth-sea alike—our world within our arms!

> –GEORGE GORDON, Lord Byron, 19th-century British poet

I could not have lived my life without Alice. If my wife had been hurt, how could I have had the strength to go on?

    –LOUIS BRANDEIS, late 19th-/early 20th-century American jurist

No man knows what the wife of his bosom is—what a ministering angel she is, until he has gone with her through the fiery trials of this world.

    –WASHINGTON IRVING, 19th-century American historian and novelist

In the future, happy occasions will come as surely as the morning. Difficult times will come as surely as night. When things go joyously, meditate according to the Buddhist tradition. When things go badly, meditate. Meditation in the manner of the Compassionate Buddha will guide your life.

    –BUDDHIST marriage homily

Deceive not thyself by overexpecting happiness in the married state . . . Look not therein for contentment greater than God will give, or a creature in this world can receive, namely, to be free from all inconveniences . . . Marriage is not like the hill of Olympus, wholly clear, without clouds.

    –THOMAS FULLER, 17th-century English author, from *The Holy State and the Profane State of Marriage*

It was an unspoken pleasure, that having come together so many years, ruined so much and repaired so little, we had endured.

    –LILLIAN HELLMAN, 20th-century American playwright

A lady of forty-seven who has been married twenty-seven years and has six children knows what love really is and described it

for me like this: "Love is what you've been through with somebody."

–JAMES THURBER, 20th-century American humorist

I always thought that there was this one perfect person for
everybody in the world and when you found that person, the
rest of the world just kind of magically faded away and the two
of you would just be inside this kind of protective bubble. But
there is no bubble. Or if there is, we have to make it. I just think life
is more than a series of moments . . . We can make choices and we
can choose to protect the people we love and that's what makes us
who we are and those are the real miracles . . . I fell in love with
you the moment I saw you . . . when I'm on my death bed, I'm
gonna know that I married the only woman I ever really loved.

–BEN (ACTOR BEN AFFLECK) in the movie *Forces of Nature*

Unity, to be real, must stand the severest strain without breaking.

–MAHATMA GANDHI, great 20th-century pacifist who led India's drive for
independence from Britain

To Mamie,
For never-failing help since 1916—in calm and in stress, in dark
days and in bright.
Love—Ike
Christmas 1955

–DWIGHT D. EISENHOWER, 34th U.S. president, in a message engraved on
a gold medallion, as a Christmas gift to his wife, December 25, 1955

A married man falling into misfortune is more apt to retrieve his
situation in the world than a single one, chiefly because his spirits are soothed and retrieved by domestic endearments, and his

self respect kept alive by finding that although all abroad be darkness and humiliation, yet there is a little world of love at home over which he is a monarch.

–BISHOP JEREMY TAYLOR, 17th-century English author and prelate

Holding It Together

Connubial happiness is a thing of too fine a texture to be handled roughly. It is a sensitive plant, which will not bear even the touch of unkindness; a delicate flower, which indifference will chill and suspicion blast. It must be watered by the showers of tender affection, expanded by the cheering glow of kindness, and guarded by the impregnable barrier of unshaken confidence. Thus matured, it will bloom with fragrance in every season of life, and sweeten even the loneliness of declining years.

–THOMAS SPRAT, 17th-/18th-century English poet

Active love is a harsh and fearful thing compared with love in dreams. Love in dreams thirsts for immediate action, quickly performed, and with everyone watching . . . Whereas active love is labor and perseverance, and for some people, perhaps, a whole science.

–FYODOR DOSTOEVSKY, 19th-century Russian novelist, from *The Brothers Karamazov*

Marriage means work, attention, care, unconditional love, acceptance of each other's imperfections, and adjustments. But if you've chosen the right partner, then nothing in your life can be more rewarding.

–JANE JACKS (ACTRESS BARBARA TARBUCK), to her son JASPER (ACTOR INGO RUDEMACHER), before his marriage to BRENDA BARRETT (ACTRESS VANESSA MARCIL) on the daytime TV drama *General Hospital,* 1996

When you have married your wife, you would think you were got upon a hill-top, and might begin to go downward by an easy slope. But you have only ended courting to begin marriage. Falling in love and winning love are often difficult tasks to over-bearing and rebellious spirits, but to keep in love is also a business of some importance, to which both man and wife must bring kindness and goodwill.

–ROBERT LOUIS STEVENSON, 19th-century Scottish novelist

It is a little embarrassing that after forty-five years of research and study, the best advice I can give to people is to be a little kinder to each other.

–ALDOUS HUXLEY, 20th-century English novelist and critic

A successful marriage is an edifice that must be rebuilt every day.

–ANDRÉ MAUROIS, French 20th-century biographer, novelist and essayist

In marriage you are chained, it is an obligation; living with someone is mutual agreement that is renegotiated and re-endorsed every day.

–BRIGITTE BARDOT, 1960s sex kitten/actress

Chains do not hold a marriage together. It is threads, hundreds of tiny threads, which sew people together through the years.

–SIMONE SIGNORET, 20th-century French actress

The web of marriage is made by propinquity, in the day-to-day living side by side, looking outward and working outward in the same direction. It is woven in space and in time of the substance of life itself.

–ANNE MORROW LINDBERGH, 20th-century American writer and the wife of aviator Charles Lindbergh, from *Gift from the Sea*

The great secret of successful marriage is to treat all disasters as incidents and none of the incidents as disasters.

–HAROLD NICHOLSON, 20th-century English biographer and diplomat

In Chota Nagput and Bengal
the betrothed are tied with threads to
mango trees, they marry the trees
as well as one another, and
the two trees marry each other.
Could we do that sometime with oaks
or beeches? This gossamer we
hold each other with, this web
of love and habit is not enough.
In mistrust of heavier ties,
I would like tree-siblings for us,
standing together somewhere, two
trees married with us, lightly, their
fingers barely touching in sleep,
our threads invisible but holding.

–WILLIAM MEREDITH, 20th-century American poet, from "Tree Marriage"

Maturity

The value of marriage is not that adults produce children, but that children produce adults.

–PETER DE VRIES, 19th-century American author

Love is a battle. Love is war. Love is growing up.

–JAMES BALDWIN, 20th-century American author, quoted in a statement by his family to the press after his death

I should like to see any kind of man, distinguishable from a gorilla, that some good and even pretty woman could not shape a husband out of.

–OLIVER WENDELL HOLMES, 19th-century American writer

We would have broken up except for the children. Who were the children? Well, she and I were.

–MORT SAHL, contemporary American comedian

Love is being stupid together.

–PAUL VALÉRY, 19th-/20th-century French poet and author

Immature love says: "I love you because I need you." Mature love says: "I need you because I love you."

–ERICH FROMM, 20th-century American psychoanalyst

The crossing of the threshold is the first step into the sacred zone of the universal source.

–JOSEPH CAMPBELL, 20th-century philosopher, from *The Hero with a Thousand Faces*

Myths and Folklore

Becky: You know it's easier to get killed by a terrorist than get married over the age of 40?

Annie: That's not true. That statistic is not true.

Becky: That's right. It's not true, but it feels true.

–BECKY (ACTRESS ROSIE O'DONNELL) and ANNIE (ACTRESS MEG RYAN), in the movie *Sleepless in Seattle*

Marry in May, repent away.
Marry in Lent, live to repent.

—ENGLISH PROVERB

Marry Monday, marry for wealth;
Marry Tuesday, marry for health;
Marry Wednesday, the best day of all;
Marry Thursday, marry for crosses;
Marry Friday, marry for losses;
Marry Saturday, no luck at all.

—OLD NURSERY RHYME

Married in white, you have chosen all right;
Married in grey, you will go far away;
Married in red, you wish yourself dead;
Married in green, ashamed to be seen;
Married in blue, he will always be true;
Married in yellow, ashamed for your fellow;
Married in brown, you will live out of town;
Married in pink, your fortune will sink.

—ANONYMOUS VICTORIAN VERSE

Marry when the year is new
Always loving, kind and true.
When February birds do mate,
You may wed, not dread your fate.
If you wed when March winds blow,
Joy and sorrow both you'll know.
Marry in April when you can,
Joy for maiden and for man.
Marry in the month of May,
You will surely rue the day.
Marry when June roses blow,

Over land and sea you'll go.
They who in July do wed,
Must labor always for their bread.
Whoever wed in August be;
Many a change are sure to see.
Marry in September's shine,
Your living will be rich and fine.
If in October you do marry,
Love will come, but riches tarry.
If you wed in bleak November,
Only joy will come, remember.
When December's snows fall fast,
Marry and true love will last.

—ANONYMOUS, "When to Marry"

. . . let the Bridegroom put the ring on the thumb of the bride, saying—In the name of the Father (on the first finger); and of the son (second finger); and of The Holy Ghost (on the third finger). Amen. And then let him leave it, because in that finger there is a certain vein which reaches to the heart.

—From the 11th-century manual for the diocese of Salisbury

Power

A man's wife has more power over him than the state has.

—RALPH WALDO EMERSON, 19th-century American poet and essayist

It's my old girl that advises. She has the head. But I never own it before her. Discipline must be maintained.

—CHARLES DICKENS, 19th-century English novelist, from *Bleak House*

Many a man that could rule a hundred millyon sthrangers with an ir'n hand is careful to take off his shoes in the front hallway whin he comes home late at night.

> –FINLEY PETER DUNNE, 20th-century American author, from *Mr. Dooley on Making a Will*

As unto the bow the cord is
So unto the man is woman,
Though she bends him, she obeys him,
Though she draws him, yet she follows,
Useless each without the other!

> –HENRY WADSWORTH LONGFELLOW, 19th-century American poet, from "The Song of Hiawatha"

Between a man and his wife nothing ought to rule but love.

> –WILLIAM PENN, founder of the state of Pennsylvania and Quaker leader

There is no realizable power that man cannot, in time, fashion the tools to attain, nor any power so secure that the naked ape will not abuse it. So it is written in the genetic cards—only physics and war hold him in check. And the wife who wants him home by five, of course.

> –*Encyclopaedia Apocryphia*

We look forward to the time when the power to love will replace the love of power. Then will our world know the blessings of peace.

> –WILLIAM GLADSTONE, 19th-century English statesman and prime minister

Because the condition of marriage is worldly and its meaning communal, no one party to it can be solely in charge. What you alone think it ought to be, it is not going to be. Where you alone think you want it to go, it is not going to go. It is going where the two of you—and marriage, time, life, history and the world—will take it.

> —WENDELL BERRY, contemporary poet and essayist, from "The Country of Marriage"

While Winston Churchill was campaigning for reelection, a voter from the other party tried to heckle him. "May we expect you to continue serving the powerful interest that controls your vote?"

Churchill growled, "I'll thank you to keep my wife's name out of this!"

> —WINSTON CHURCHILL, Britain's prime minister, 1940–1945; 1951–1955

Surprise

Marriage is a continuous process of getting used to things you hadn't expected.

> —ANONYMOUS

In my church, marriage is like a box of chocolates, you never know what you're going to get!

> —REVEREND SUN MYUNG MOON, head of the Unification Church (known for presiding over mass marriages of 30,000), speaking at the double wedding of his son and daughter

Try praising your wife, even if it does frighten her at first.

> —BILLY SUNDAY, 19th-/20th-century American evangelist

The most welcome surprise you can give your wife on your anniversary is to remember it.

> —ANONYMOUS

He who marries is like the Doge (of Venice) who marries the Adriatic—he doesn't know what's in it: treasures, pearls, monsters, unknown storms.

–HEINRICH HEINE, 19th-century German poet

No one worth possessing
Can be quite possessed.

–SARA TEASDALE, 19th-/20th-century American poet

One should never know too precisely whom one has married.

–FRIEDRICH NIETZSCHE, 19th-century German philosopher

Chapter 3

For Richer or for Poorer

Values

A heaven on earth I have won by wooing thee.

> –WILLIAM SHAKESPEARE, 16th-/17th-century English poet and playwright

For thy sweet love remember'd such wealth brings,
That then I scorn to change my state with kings.

> –WILLIAM SHAKESPEARE, 16th-/17th-century English poet and playwright, from Sonnet XXIX

No matter how much money you have, you've got nothing if you can't trust somebody as close to you as I am.

> –LOUISE BROWN (ACTRESS JULIANNA MARGULIES) in the movie, *Newton Boys*

I'd lose it anyway. Just give me a bread tie.

> –MINDY MCCREADY, country singer, discussing the ring that helped seal
> her marriage to Superman (ACTOR DEAN CAIN, star of the TV series *Lois
> and Clark*)

In marriage do thou be wise: Prefer the person before money,
virtue before beauty, the mind before the body; then thou hast a
wife, a friend, a companion, a second self.

> –WILLIAM PENN, founder of Pennsylvania and Quaker leader

Choose a wife by your ear than your eye.

> –THOMAS FULLER, 17th-century English author

Look for a sweet person. Forget rich.

> –ESTEE LAUDER, 20th-century American cosmetics tycoon

No woman marries for money; they are all clever enough, before
marrying a millionaire, to fall in love with him first.

> –CESARE PAVESE, 20th-century Italian writer

A wise lover values
not so much
the gift of the lover
as the love of the giver.

> –THOMAS À KEMPIS, 14th-/15th-century German ecclesiastical writer

You can't appreciate home till you've left it, money till it's spent,
your wife till she's joined a woman's club.

> –O. HENRY, 19th-/20th-century American writer, from *Roads of Destiny,
> the Fourth in Salvador*

Whoever lives true life will love true life.

> –ELIZABETH BARRETT BROWNING, 19th-century British poet known for her
> great love affair with her husband, Robert Browning

In vain is that man born fortunate, if he be unfortunate in his marriage.

—ANNE DACIER, 18th-century French poet

My boat is of ebony,
The holes in my flute are golden.

As a plant takes out stains from silk
So wine takes sadness from the heart.

When one has good wine,
A graceful boat,
And a maiden's love
Why envy the immortal gods?

—LI TAI-PO, 8th-century Chinese poet, "Song on the River"

If thou must love me, let it be for naught
Except for love's sake only. Do not say,
"I love her for her smile—her look—her way—
Of speaking gently,—for a trick of thought
That falls in well with mine, and certes brought
A sense of pleasant ease on such a day"—
For these things in themselves, Beloved, may
Be changed, or change for thee,—and love, so wrought,
May be unwrought so. Neither love me for
Thine own dear pity's wiping my cheeks dry,—
A creature might forget to weep, who bore
Thy comfort long, and lose thy love thereby!
But love me for love's sake, that evermore
Thou mayest love on, through love's eternity.

—ELIZABETH BARRETT BROWNING, 19th-century British poet known for her great love affair with her husband, Robert Browning, from "Sonnets from the Portuguese"

The moral man will find the moral law beginning in the relation between husband and wife, but ending only in the vast reaches of the universe.

> –CONFUCIUS, 6th-century, B.C., Chinese philosopher, founder of Confucianism

I don't want to be worshipped. I want to be loved.

> –TRACEY LORD (ACTRESS KATHARINE HEPBURN), in the movie *Philadelphia Story*

. . . *And Lack Thereof*

I want a wedding at the Waldorf
With Champagne and caviar.
I want a wedding like the Vanderbilts' had,
Everything big, not small.
If I can't have that kind of wedding,
I don't want to get married at all.

> –AMERICAN FOLK SONG

It isn't that I give a hoot about jewelry. Except diamonds, of course.

> –HOLLY GOLIGHTLY (ACTRESS AUDREY HEPBURN), in the movie *Breakfast at Tiffany's*

All my life, ever since I was a little girl, I've always had the same dream—to marry a zillionaire.

> –LOCO (ACTRESS BETTY GRABLE), warming to the husband-snagging scheme in the movie *How to Marry a Millionaire*

The only sort of man most women want to marry is the fella with a will of his own—made out in her favor.

> –BRENDAN BEHAN, 20th-century Irish playwright and author

No longer will I play the field. The field stinks . . . both econom-
ically and socially.

> –HOLLY GOLIGHTLY (ACTRESS AUDREY HEPBURN), in the movie *Breakfast at
> Tiffany's*

Sharing the Wealth

This is the miracle that happens every time to those who really
love; the more they give, the more they possess.

> –RAINER MARIA RILKE, 19th-/20th-century German poet

Yet I would not have all yet.
He that hath all can have no more;
And since my love doth every day admit
New growth, thou shouldst have new rewards in store;
Thou canst not every day give me thy heart.
If thou canst give it, then thou never gavest it;
Love's riddles are, that though thy heart depart,
It stays at home, and thou with losing savest it:
But we will have a way more liberal
Than changing hearts, to join them; so we shall
Be one, and one another's all.

> –JOHN DONNE, 16th-/17th-century English poet and clergyman

A man who wants a happy marriage should learn to keep his
mouth shut and his checkbook open.

> –GROUCHO MARX, 20th-century American actor and comedian

Ne'er take a wife till thou hast a house (and a fire) to put her in.

> –BENJAMIN FRANKLIN, 18th-century American patriot, diplomat, author,
> printer, scientist and inventor

Give all in love;
Obey thy heart;
Friends, kindred, days,
Estate, good fame,
Plans, credit, and the Muse,
Nothing refuse.

'Tis a brave master,
Let it have scope:
Follow it utterly,
Hope beyond hope:
High and more high
It dives into noon,
With wing unspent
Untold intent;
But it is a god,
Knows its own path
And the outlets of the sky.

It was never for the mean;
It requireth courage stout.
Souls above doubt,
Valor unbending. It will reward,
They shall return
More than they were,
And ever ascending . . .
Give all in love

> –RALPH WALDO EMERSON, 19th-century American poet and essayist, from
> "Give All in Love"

Love ever gives,
Forgives, outlives,
And ever stands
With open hands.

And, while it lives,
It gives.
For this is Love's prerogative—
To give and give and give.

> –JOHN OXENHAM, 19th-/20th-century English poet

If I were a king what would
   I do?
I'd make you a queen, for I'd
   Marry you.

> –VERSE FROM A VICTORIAN CARD

The only gift is a portion of thyself.

> –RALPH WALDO EMERSON, 19th-century American poet and essayist, from
> *Essay: Second Series. Gifts.*

Success

Success in marriage is much more than finding the right person;
it is a matter of being the right person.

> –B. R. BRICKNER

Every man who is happy is a successful man even if he has failed
in everything else.

> –WILLIAM LYON PHELPS, 19th-/20th-century American writer, critic and
> educator

Won 1880. One 1884.

> –WILLIAM JENNINGS BRYAN, 19th-/20th-century American lawyer and
> politician, from an inscription on a ring he gave his wife

My most brilliant achievement was my ability to persuade my wife to marry me.

–Winston Churchill, Britain's prime minister, 1940–45; 1950–55

The crowning glory of loving and being loved is that the pair make no real progress; however far they have advanced into the enchanted land during the day they must start again from the frontier the next morning.

–James Barrie, 19th-/20th-century Scottish novelist and playwright

One doesn't have to get anywhere in marriage. It's not a public conveyance.

–Iris Murdoch, 20th-century English novelist

I have enjoyed the happiness of this world; I have lived and loved.

–Friedrich von Schiller, 19th-/20th-century German dramatist and writer

An immature person may achieve great success in a career but never in marriage.

–Benjamin Spock, American physician and writer

Every man who is high up loves to think he has done it all himself; and the wife smiles, and lets it go at that. It's only our joke. Every woman knows that.

–Sir James Barrie, 19th-/20th-century Scottish novelist and playwright

Chapter 4

In Sickness and In Health

Healthy Habits

One of the best things about marriage is that it gets young people to bed at a decent hour.

> –M. M. MUSSELMAN, 20th-century American playwright

Growth

We are shaped and fashioned by what we love.

> –JOHANN WOLFGANG VON GOETHE, 18th-/19th-century German poet and dramatist

When a person is in love, he seems to himself wholly changed from what he was before; and he fancies that everybody sees him in the same light. This is a great mistake; but reason being obscured by passion, he cannot be convinced, and goes on still under the delusion . . .

> —Blaise Pascal, 17th-century French mathematician and philosopher
> from *On the Passion of the Soul,* translated by George Pearce

I harbor within—we all do—a vision of my highest self, a dream of what I could and should become. May I pursue this vision, labor to make real my dream. Thus will I give meaning to my life.

> —From the Reform Jewish Prayer Book *Gates of Prayer: The New Union Prayer Book*

I want to get married. I've always wanted to get married. If I can get married, it means I've changed. I'm a new person.

> —Muriel (actress Toni Collette) explaining her dream of marriage as an escape from her past, in the movie *Muriel's Wedding*

I love you, not for what you are, but for what
I am when I am with you. I love you, not
only for what you have made of yourself, but
for what you are making of me. I love
you for the part of me that you bring out; I love
you for putting your hand into my heaped-up
heart and passing over all the foolish, weak
things that you can't help dimly seeing there,
and for drawing out into the lights all the
beautiful belongings that no one else had
looked quite far enough to find. I love you
because you are helping me to make of the
lumber of my life not a tavern but a temple;
out of the works of my every day, not a
reproach, but a song. I love you because
you have done more than any creed could

have done to make me good, and more
than any fate could have done to make
me happy. You have done it without
a touch, without a word, without a sign.
you have done it by being yourself.
perhaps that is what being in love
means, after all.

> —ROY CROFT, "Love," from *Best Loved Poems of the American People*

It is a lovely thing to have a husband and wife developing together. That is what marriage really means: helping one another to reach the full status of being persons, responsible and autonomous beings who do not run away from life.

> —PAUL TOURNIER, contemporary author specializing in psychological themes

Love alone is capable of uniting living beings in such a way as to complete and fulfill them, for it alone takes them and joins them by what is deepest in themselves.

> —PIERRE TEILHARD DE CHARDIN, 19th-/20th-century philosopher and priest, from *The Phenomenon of Man*

Do you think it is easy to change?
Ah, it is very hard to change and be different.
It means passing through the waters of oblivion.

> —D. H. LAWRENCE, 19th-/20th-century English writer, from *Change*

Blessed are the man and the woman
who have grown beyond themselves . . .

> —PSALM I, *A Book of Psalms,* adapted by Stephen Mitchell

[Love] . . . is a high inducement to the individual to ripen, to become something in himself, to become world, to become world for himself for another's sake, it is a great exacting claim upon him, something that chooses him out and calls him to vast things. Only in this sense, as the task of working at themselves ("to hearken and to hammer day and night") might young people use the love that is given them.

> –RAINER MARIA RILKE, 19th-/20th-century German poet, from *Letters to a Young Poet*

Love is not a possession but a growth.

> –HENRY WARD BEECHER, 19th-century American clergyman

A person's character is but half formed till after wedlock.

> –C. SIMMONS

"There is an advantage to being married," said the husband on his thirtieth anniversary. "You can't make a fool of yourself without knowing it quickly."

> –ANONYMOUS

He that has not got a Wife, is not yet a complete man.

> –BENJAMIN FRANKLIN, 18th-century American patriot, diplomat, author, printer, scientist and inventor, from *Poor Richard's Almanac,* 1733

A man in love is incomplete until he is married.

> –ZSA ZSA GABOR, glam queen and actress, known for her plethora of husbands (sequentially, that is)

Love in a Time of Sickness

I was wearing a hospital gown.

> –LARRY KING, TV talk show host, commenting on his attire for his (seventh) wedding, this one to Shawn Southwick, held in his hospital room as he recovered from angioplasty

Love cures people, both the ones who give it and the ones who receive it.

> –DR. KARL MENNINGER, 19th-/20th-century American psychiatrist and writer

Chapter 5

'Til Death Do You Part

Forever Love

To every thing there is a season, and a time to every purpose under the heaven:

A time to be born, and a time to die; a time to plant, and a time to pluck up that which is planted;

A time to kill, and a time to heal; a time to break down, and a time to build up;

A time to weep, and a time to laugh; a time to mourn, and a time to dance;

A time to cast away stones, and a time to gather stones together; a time to embrace, and a time to refrain from embracing;

A time to get, and a time to lose; a time to keep, and a time to cast away;

A time to rend, and a time to sew; a time to keep silence, and a time to speak;

A time to love, and a time to hate; a time of war, and a time of peace.

—ECCLESIASTES 3:1–8, *The Holy Bible,* King James version

... true love is a durable fire,
In the mind ever burning,
Never sick, never old, never dead,
From itself never turning.

> –SIR WALTER RALEGH, English 16th-/17th-century explorer, from "As You
> Came From the Holy Land"

God with honour hang your head,
Groom, and grace you, bride, your bed
With lissome scions, sweet scions,
Out of hallowed bodies bred.

Each be other's comfort kind:
Deep, deeper than divined,
Divine charity, dear charity,
Fast you ever, fast bind.

Then let the march tread our ears:
I to him turn with tears
Who to wedlock, his wonder wedlock,
Deals triumph and immortal years.

> –GERARD MANLEY HOPKINS, 19th-century English poet, from "At the Wed-
> ding March"

I want to wake up with you every morning and fall asleep next
to you every night. I want to laugh and dream and fight and
make up. I want to make babies, mistakes, music, and magic to
really live. All with you. And in fifty years or so, when Death
comes to take me, I want you right there fighting for me with all
that ferocious love in your heart, telling Death, "No! It's too
soon! It's too soon."

> –MAX HOLDEN (ACTOR JAMES DePAIVA), during his marriage ceremony to
> his TV wife, Luna Moody (ACTRESS SUSAN BATTEN), on the daytime TV
> drama One Life to Live, 1993

What greater thing is there for two human souls than to feel that they are joined for life—to strengthen each other in all labor, to rest on each other in all sorrow, to minister to each other in all pain, to be one with each other in silent unspeakable memories at the moment of the last parting.

    –GEORGE ELIOT, 19th-century English novelist

. . . our life reminds me
of a forest in which there is a graceful clearing
and in that opening a house,
an orchard and garden,
comfortable shades, and flowers . . .
The forest is mostly dark, its ways
to be made anew day after day, the dark
richer than the light and more blessed,
provided we stay brave
enough to keep on going in . . .

    –WENDELL BERRY, contemporary poet and essayist, from "The Country of
      Marriage"

I do not offer the old smooth prizes,
But offer rough new prizes,
These are the days that must happen to you:
You shall not heap up what is called riches,
You shall scatter with lavish hands all that you earn or achieve.
However sweet the laid-up stores,
However convenient the dwellings,
You shall not remain there.
However sheltered the port,
And however calm the waters,
You shall not anchor there.
However welcome the hospitality that welcomes you

You are permitted to receive it but a little while
Afoot and lighthearted, take to the open road,
Healthy, free, the world before you,
The long brown path before you, leading wherever you choose.
Say only to one another:
Comrade, I give you my hand!
I give you my love, more precious than money,
I give you myself before preaching or law:
Will you give me yourself?
Will you come travel with me?
Shall we stick by each other as long as we live?

> –WALT WHITMAN, 19th-century American poet from "Song of the Open Road"

And Ruth said, Intreat me not to leave thee, or to return from following after thee: for whither thou goest, I will go; and where thou lodgest, I will lodge: thy people shall be my people, and thy God my God:

Where thou diest, will I die, and there will I be buried: the LORD do so to me, and more also, if ought but death part thee and me.

> –RUTH 1:16–17, *The Holy Bible,* King James version

Thrice joyous are those united by an unbroken band of love, unsundered by any division before life's final day.

> –HORACE, 1st-century, B.C., Roman satirist and poet

Some people do spend their whole lives together.

> –ANNA SCOTT (ACTRESS JULIA ROBERTS), in the movie *Notting Hill*

Will you love me in December as you do in May?
Will you love me in the good old-fashioned way?

> –JAMES J. WALKER

Grow old along with me!
The best is yet to be.
The last of life, for which the first was made.
Our times are in His hand.
Who saith, A whole I planned,
Youth shows but half. Trust God, see all, nor be afraid!

> –ROBERT BROWNING, 19th-century English poet, known for his great love affair with his wife, Elizabeth Barrett Browning, from "Rabbi Ben Ezra"

Marriage is the permanent conversation between two people who talk over everything and everyone until death breaks the record.

> –CYRIL CONNOLLY, British 20th-century author

This is for the rest of your life. Finally, you've got to marry the person you love with your whole heart.

> –DAVID (ACTOR DAVID BOWER), objecting to the ceremony-in-progress on the grounds that the groom loves someone other than the bride, in the movie *Four Weddings and a Funeral*

. . . Here upon earth, we are Kings, and non be wee
Can be such Kings, nor of the such subjects bee.
Who is so safe as wee? where none can doe
Treason to us, expect one of us two.
  True and false fears let us refraine,
Let us love nobly, and live, and adde againe
Yeares and yeares unto yeares, till we attaine
To write threescore . . .

> –JOHN DONNE, 16th-/17th-century English poet and clergyman, from "The Anniversary"

. . . forever, we said
toasting ourselves in an empty house

And who did we marry?

I married the moon
I married my silver remotest self

she married the mirror
she married an echo of ravishing kisses

. . .

we didn't care who paid the bills
we didn't care who swept the floor

we had the moon, we had the mirror
we smelted silver in echoing kisses

forever, we said
holding hands on the street

–DOROTHY PORTER, 20th-century poet, from "Wives"

If you knew what I went through. If you knew how much I loved you. If you knew how much I still love you.

–ILSA LUND LASZLO (ACTRESS INGRID BERGMAN) to Rick Blaine (ACTOR HUMPHREY BOGART), in the movie *Casablanca*

So let our love
As endless prove,
And pure as gold forever.

–ROBERT HERRICK, 17th-century English poet, from "To Julia"

'TIL DEATH DO YOU PART

I would ask of you, my darling,
   A question soft and low,
That gives me many a heartache
   As the moments come and go.

Your love I know is truthful,
   But the truest love grows cold;
It is this that I would ask you:
   Will you love me when I'm old?

Life's morn will soon be waning,
   And its evening bells be tolled,
But my heart shall know no sadness,
   If you'll love me when I'm old.
Down the stream of life together
   We are sailing side by side,
Hoping some bright day to anchor
   Safe beyond the surging tide.
Today our sky is cloudless,
   But the night may clouds unfold;
But, though storms may gather round us,
   Will you love me when I'm old?

When my hair shall shade the snowdrift,
   And mine eyes shall dimmer grow
I would lean upon some loved one,
   Through the valley as I go.
I would claim of you a promise,
   Worth to me a world of gold;
It is only this, my darling,
   That you'll love me when I'm old.

             –ANONYMOUS

You will never age for me, nor fade, nor die.

> —WILL SHAKESPEARE (ACTOR JOSEPH FIENNES) to Lady Violet (actress
> Gwyneth Paltrow), in the movie *Shakespeare in Love*

Thus let me hold thee to my heart,
And every care resign:
And we shall never, never part,
My life—my all that's mine!

> —OLIVER GOLDSMITH, 18th-century Anglo-Irish playwright, novelist and
> poet

A certain sort of talent is almost indispensable for people who would spend years together and not bore themselves to death . . . To dwell happily together, they should be versed in the niceties of the heart, and born with a faculty for willing compromise . . . Should laugh over the same sort of jest and have many . . . an old joke between them which time cannot wither nor custom stale . . . You could read Kant by yourself if you wanted, but you must share a joke with someone else.

> —ROBERT LOUIS STEVENSON, 19th-century Scottish novelist, from *Virginibus
> Puerisque*

Your wedding-ring wears thin, dear wife; ah,
    summers not a few,
Since I put it on your finger first, have passed
    o'er me and you;
And, love what changes we have seen,—what
    cares and pleasures, too,
Since you became my own dear wife, when this old ring was
    new!

The past is dear, its sweetness still our memories
    treasure yet;
The griefs we've borne, together borne, we would
    not now forget.
Whatever, wife, the future brings, heart unto
    heart still true,
We'll share as we have shared all else since this
    old ring was new.

    –WILLIAM COX BENNETT, 19th-century English journalist, from "The Worn
      Wedding Ring"

We've been together now for forty years
An' it don't seem a day too long.

    –ALBERT CHERAKER

He came into my life as the warm wind of spring had awakened
flowers, as the April showers awaken the earth. My love for him
was an unchanging love, high and deep, free and faithful, strong
as death. Each year I learned to love him more and more. I think
of the days and years we spent together with gratitude, for God
has been kind and generous in letting me love him.

    –ANNA CHENNAULT, 20th-century American writer

My love is so strong that it can only be overcome by death, and
if, which God forbid, you should die before me, my heart shall
remain dead for every other, and my mind and affection shall
follow you to eternity, there to dwell with you . . .
    "He does not wait too long who waits for something good." I
hope, by God's blessing, that it is a good thing we both are waiting for.

    –QUEEN CHRISTINA OF SWEDEN to Prince Karl Gustaff, January 5, 1644

I long to believe in immortality. I shall never be ab[le] to bid you
an entire farewell. If I am destined to be happy with you here—
how short is the longest Life—I wish to believe in immortality—
I wish to live with you forever . . .

> –JOHN KEATS, 19th-century English poet, in a letter to Fanny Brawne
> dated June 1820

The memories of long love
Gather like drifting snow,
Poignant as the mandarin ducks,
Who float side by side in sleep.

. . .

Falling from the ridge
Of high Tsukuba
The Minano River
At last gathers itself,
Like my love, into
A deep, still pool.

> –KENNETH REXROTH, 20th-century American poet, from *One Hundred Po-
> ems from the Japanese*

What thou lovest well remains,
the rest is dross . . .

–EZRA POUND, 20th-century American poet, from "Cantos"

The time-span of *union* is eternity,
This life is a jar, and in it, union is the pure wine.
If we aren't together, of what use is the jar?

> –JALĀL AL-DĪN RŪMĪ, 13th-century Persian poet

Shall I compare thee to a summer's day?
Thou art more lovely and more temperate:
Rough winds do shake the darling buds of May,
And summer's lease hath all too short a date:

Sometimes too hot the eye to heaven shines,
And often in his gold complexion dimm'd,
And every fair from air sometime declines,
By chance, or nature's changing course, untrim'd
But thy eternal summer shall not fade,
Nor loose possession of that fair thou ow'st,
Nor shall death brag thou wandr'st in his shade,
When in eternal lines to time thou grow'st
    So long as men can breath, or eyes can see,
    So long lives this, and this gives life to thee.

> —WILLIAM SHAKESPEARE, 16th-/17th-century English poet and playwright,
> Sonnet XVII

You say, to me-wards your affection's strong;
Pray love me little, so you love me long.
Slowly goes farre: The meane is best: Desire
Grown violent, do's either die, or tire.

> —ROBERT HERRICK, 17th-century English poet, from "Love Me Little, Love
> Me Long"

I love you. I want to be together all the time. When I think about
us, I am thinking about forever.

> —WILLIS NEWTON (ACTOR MATTHEW MCCONAUGHEY), in the movie *Newton
> Boys*

We have lived and loved together
    Through many changing years;
We have shared each other's gladness
    And wept each other's tears;
I have known ne'er a sorrow
    That was long unsoothed by thee;
For thy smiles can make a summer
    Where darkness else would be.

Like the leaves that fall around us
   In autumn's fading hours,
Are the traitor's smiles, that darken
   When the cloud of sorrow lowers;
And though many such we've known, love,
   Too prone, alas, to range,
We both can speak of one love
   Which time can never change.

We have lived and loved together
   Through many changing years,
We have shared each other's gladness
   And wept each other's tears.
And let us hope the future,
   As the past has been will be:
I will share with thee my sorrows,
   And thou thy joys with me.

> —CHARLES JEFFREYS, 19th-century English writer, from "We Have Lived
> and Loved Together"

If you should go before me, dear, walk slowly
Down the ways of death, well-worn and wide . . .

> —ADELAIDE LOVE, 20th-century American poet, from "Walk Slowly"

Believe me, if all those endearing young charms,
   Which I gaze on so fondly today,
Were to change by tomorrow, and fleet in my arms,
   Like fairy gifts fading away,
Thou wouldst still be adored, as this moment thou art,
   Let thy loveliness fade as it will,
And around the dear ruin each wish of my heart
   Would entwine itself verdantly still.

It is not while beauty and youth are thine own,
   And thy cheeks unprofaned by a tear,
That the fervor and faith of a soul may be known,
   To which time will but make thee more dear;
No, the heart that has truly loved never forgets,
   But as truly loves on to the close,
As the sun-flower turns on her god, when he sets,
   The same look which she turned when he rose.

> –THOMAS MOORE, 18th-/19th-century Irish poet, from "Believe Me, if All
> Those Endearing Young Charms"

Only our love hath no decay;
This, no tomorrow hath, nor yesterday,
Running it never runs from us away,
But truly keeps his first, last, everlasting day.

> –JOHN DONNE, 16th-/17th-century English poet, "Only Our Love"

Heaven will be
no heaven to me
if I do not
meet my wife there.

> –ANDREW JACKSON, 7th U.S. president

Two lovers by a moss-grown spring;
They leaned soft cheeks together there,
Mingled the dark and sunny hair,
And heard the wooing thrushes sing.
   O budding time!
   O love's blest prime!

Two wedded from the portal stept;
The bells made happy carollings,

The air was soft as fanning wings,
White petals on the pathway slept.
    O pure-eyed bride!
    O tender pride!

Two faces o'er a cradle bent:
Two hands above the head were locked;
These pressed each other while they rocked,
Those watched a life that love had sent.
    O solemn hour!
    O hidden power!

Two parents by the even fire;
The red light fell about their knees
On heads that rose by slow degrees
Like buds upon the lily spire.
    O patient life!
    O tender strife!

The two still sat together there,
The red light shone about their knees;
But all the heads by slow degrees
Had gone and left that lonely pair.
    O voyage fast!
    O vanished past!

The red light shone upon the floor
And made the space between them wide;
They drew their chairs up side by side,
Their pale cheeks joined, and said, Once more!
    O memories!
    O past that is!

    —GEORGE ELIOT, 19th-century English novelist

It's Better When You're Older

As your wedding ring wears,
You'll wear off your cares.

> –THOMAS FULLER, 17th-century English author

Dawn love is silver,
   Wait for the west;
Old love is gold love—
   Old love is best.

> –KATHERINE LEE BATES, 19th-/20th-century American educator

Young love is a flame, very pretty, often very hot and fierce, but still only light and flickering. The love of the older and disciplined heart is as coals, deep-burning, unquenchable.

> –HENRY WARD BEECHER, 19th-century American clergyman

The bonds of marriage are like any other bonds—they mature slowly.

> –PETER DE VRIES, 20th-century writer and editor

Love seems the swiftest, but it is the slowest of all growths. No man or woman really knows what perfect love is until they have been married a quarter of a century.

> –MARK TWAIN, 19th-century American writer

The love we have in our youth is superficial compared to the love that an old man has for his old wife.

> –WILL DURANT, 20th-century American historian

It takes years to marry completely two hearts, even the most loving and well assorted. A happy wedlock is a long falling in love.
Young persons think love belongs only to the brown-haired and
crimson-cheeked. So it does for its beginning. But the golden marriage is a part of love which the Bridal day knows nothing of . . .

–THEODORE PARKER, 19th-century American clergyman

The relation of romantic love to married love is somewhat like
that of a little tree to the larger tree which it later becomes. It has
life and fresh young energy that enables it to grow. When it has
grown into a larger tree its heart and vitality are still there but,
with continued life, it has taken new rings of growth, its branches
have spread wider and its roots have gone deeper. Moreover it
bears flowers and fruit which the little tree did not produce.

–LELAND FOSTER WOOD, writer, from *How Love Grows in Marriage*

I believe the second half of one's life is meant to be better than
the first half. The first half is finding out how you do it. And the
second half is enjoying it.

–FRANCES LEAR, founder and editor of *Lear's Magazine,* the first U.S. magazine geared toward women over 40

It's a long time ago, my darling, but the 33 years have been really
profitable to us, and is worth more each year than it was the year
before. And so it will be always, dearest old Sweetheart of my
youth.

Good night and sleep well.

–MARK TWAIN, 19th-century American writer in a note sent up to his
wife's room in Italy where she lay seriously ill

True love is the ripe fruit of a lifetime.

> —ALPHONSE DE LAMARTINE, 19th-century French poet

Such a large sweet fruit is a comfortable marriage, that it needs a very long summer to ripen in and then a long winter to mellow and sweeten in.

> —THEODORE PARKER, 19th-century American clergyman

In the marriage ceremony, that moment when falling in love is replaced by the arduous dream of staying in love, the words "in sickness and in health, for richer, for poorer, till death do us part" set love in the temporal context in which it achieves its meaning. As time begins to elapse, one begins to love the other because they have shared the same experience . . . Selves may not intertwine; but lives do, and shared memory becomes as much of a bond as the bond of the flesh . . .

> —MICHAEL IGNATIEFF, from "Lodged in the Heart and Memory"

No, I haven't any formula. I can just say it's been a very happy experience . . . a successful marriage, I think, gets happier as the years go by.

> —DWIGHT D. EISENHOWER, 34th U.S. president, on his forty-third wedding anniversary

A marriage begins by joining man and wife together, but this relationship between two people, however deep at the time, needs to develop and mature with the passing years. For that it must be held firm in the web of family relationships between parents and children, between grandparents and grandchildren, between cousins, aunts and uncles.

> —QUEEN ELIZABETH II of Great Britain

The world rolls; the circumstances vary every hour ... [The lovers'] once flaming regard is sobered ... and losing in violence what it gains in extent, it becomes a thorough good understanding. At last [the lovers] discover that all which at first drew them together—those once sacred features, that magical play of charms—had a prospective end, like the scaffolding by which the house was built, and the purification of the intellect and the heart, from year to year, is the real marriage ...

> –RALPH WALDO EMERSON, 19th-century American poet and essayist, from his essay "Love"

Many husbands and wives, I believe, make the mistake of expecting too much early in marriage, and then of expecting too little later on.

> –DAVID R. MACE, 20th-century Scottish sociologist

This is a great day, my darling, the day that gave you to me fifteen years ago. You were very precious to me then, you are still more precious to me now. In having each other then, we were well off, but poor compared to what we have now with the children. I kiss you, my darling wife—and those little rascals.

> –MARK TWAIN, 19th-century American writer in a note to his wife

I am now I believe fixed at this Seat with an agreeable Consort for Life and hope to find more happiness in retirement than I ever experienced amidst a wide and bustling World.

> –GEORGE WASHINGTON, 1st U.S. president, September 20, 1759, Mount Vernon

. . . *Or Not*

"Do you think the romance has gone out of our lives?"
"Burp."

> —MARGE SIMPSON and husband Homer, in the animated television series *The Simpsons*

At the end of what is called the "sexual life," the only love which has lasted is the love which has everything, every disappointment, every failure, and every betrayal, which has accepted even the sad fact that in the end there is no desire so deep as the simple desire for companionship.

> —GRAHAM GREENE, contemporary English novelist

Wives are young men's mistresses, companions for middle age, and old men's nurses.

> —FRANCIS BACON, 16th-/17th-century English author, from *Essays of Marriage and Single Life.*

At her fiftieth wedding anniversary, the wife was asked if she had ever thought of divorcing her husband. "Divorce him? No. Shoot him—yes!"

> —ANONYMOUS

Later, it's a different question—ah yes, later men take to marriage like you'd take to a comfy country sofa . . . but by then women are screaming and knocking them over in the rush to flee Bluebeard's dungeon.

> —ANNA MARIA DELL'OSO, contemporary Australian feminist writer

The true one of youth's love, [will] prove a faithful help-meet in those years when the dream of life is over, and we live in its re-alities.

–ROBERT SOUTHEY, 18th-/19th-century English poet

Ma used to say love is kinda like the measles. You only get it once. The older you are, the tougher it goes.

–ADAM (ACTOR HOWARD KEEL) offering advice on love and marriage, in the movie *Seven Brides for Seven Brothers*

The best way to get husbands to do something is to suggest that perhaps they are too old to do it.

–SHIRLEY MACLAINE, contemporary American actress

Husband and wife come to look alike at last.

–OLIVER WENDELL HOLMES, 19th-century American writer

Like a prune, you are not getting any better looking, but you are getting sweeter.

–N. D. SICE

Whatever you may look like, marry a man your own age—as your beauty fades, so will his eyesight.

–PHYLLIS DILLER, contemporary American comedian

Love Keeps You Young

Love makes those young whom age doth chill
And whom he finds young, keeps young still.

–WILLIAM CARTWRIGHT, 17th-century English poet, from "To Chloe"

Age does not protect you from love, but love to some extent protects you from age.

—JEANNE MOREAU, contemporary French actress

The heart that loves is always young.

—GREEK PROVERB

True love is eternal, infinite, and always like itself. It is equal and pure . . . and always young in the heart.

—HONORÉ DE BALZAC, 19th-century French novelist

Part 2

How to Say It

Chapter 6

Pre-Wedding Parties

You can make your wedding speak for you long before the actual wedding day. From the shower to the rehearsal dinner, there are dozens of ways to incorporate quotes, quips, poetry and prose into your pre-wedding parties to help establish the uniqueness of the pending event.

∽ The Wedding Shower ∽

At a traditional bridal shower, friends and family "showered" the bride with homemaking "essentials," everything from linens to lingerie. The idea was that the bride was finally moving out of her parents' house and needed to stock up. Today, when so many people live alone (or together) for years before marriage, showers are taking a more creative turn—your friends might throw you a couples shower (men and women come, including your fiancé), a sports shower, a pampering shower, a travel shower, or a "words of love" shower. Here's how:

SHOWER HER WITH WORDS

Top Tips for Including Quotes in Your Wedding Shower:

Get Plied with Poetic Presents

Instead of presenting you with supplies to stock your house, guests at *your* shower will bring gifts to stock your heart. The shower hosts might include a line on the invitation about your shower theme, such as, "Shower Her with Words of Love." (They can explain further when guests call to RSVP.) Guests might give the complete sonnets of William Shakespeare, a compilation of love songs on CD, a set of the world's most romantic movies on tape, a collection of romance novels or a piece of jewelry engraved with a romantic quote.

Play Language Games

Why stick to those traditional shower games when you can create your own, using the world's most romantic words?

Sample Shower Games

Limerick Slam

Party hosts choose the first line from a poem or a quip from this book. Each guest writes a limerick relating to your relationship, starting with that line. The limerick might start with: *"Sexiness wears thin and beauty fades."* (JOANNE WOODWARD, WORDS ABOUT HUSBANDS) Guests complete the limerick, writing something about longevity, constancy, commitment, etc. For example, a guest might write:

Sexiness wears thin and beauty fades,
Love matures like growing grass blades.
But don't you fret
You're not old yet.
Marriage is time for at-home panty raids.

Good headings to look under include, "Compromise, Tolerance and Lack Thereof," "Forever Love," "Constancy" or "It's Better When You're Older."

Poetry Reading

You could make it an afternoon of poetry. Give your guests a chance to choose one piece each from the book that they think speaks about your relationship or about their own ideas of love. Take turns reading aloud.

Romantic Charades

Instead of movie titles, act out short quips or poetry fragments from this book. You might try lines such as: *One good husband is worth two good wives* (BENJAMIN FRANKLIN, WORDS ABOUT HUSBANDS); and *Love is the answer* (WOODY ALLEN, SEX). Party hosts can jot down lines to use ahead of time, making sure to keep the quotes and quote fragments short and snappy. Or pass the book around and let guests choose their own.

Say It with Food

For lunch, feed their bodies and minds. Serve alphabet soup, followed by a heart-shaped cake cut in two and frosted as two half-hearts. Top with these words (in icing): *Marriage is the fusion of two hearts, the union of two lives* (PETER MARSHALL, SOUL MATES/SYNERGY) Put bowls of candy conversation hearts on the tables. Print up a shower menu with a quote on the top.

❧ The Rehearsal Dinner ❧

Unlike the wedding itself (at which half your guests may be parents' friends), the rehearsal dinner usually includes only those closest to you—your immediate family, your wedding party (and spouses and parents of underage members), your officiant (and spouse) and out-of-town guests. Because it's more personal, and often more casual, the rehearsal dinner is a perfect time to tell others how you really feel—with a little help from the experts, of course.

SPICE IT UP WITH WORDS

Top Tips for Including Quotes in Your Rehearsal Dinner:

Give Toasts That Talk

Because it's a small, intimate group, your toasts can be longer, more creative, and more revealing than during your wedding reception. Turn to Chapter 8 for tips on writing great toasts.

Time for Toasts

At a rehearsal dinner, the toasting order usually goes like this:

- Toasts to the bride and groom:
  Groom's dad, best man, maid of honor, other friends

- Toasts by the bride and groom:
  Groom toasts bride, parents, new parents, friends. Bride toasts groom, parents, new parents, friends.

- Dual toast:
  Bride and groom toast anyone they wish to honor, as a unit.

Give Readings

The rehearsal dinner is a perfect time to read a short passage or poem that expresses your thoughts about your pending marriage or about those gathered around you. You might also ask members of your wedding party or family to look through this book for a reading that helps say what they feel. (Turn to Chapter 7 for help choosing readings)

Stage a Scene

If your wedding party is a talented crew, considering having them stage a short play that relates to your wedding or to how you met. It can be something from a popular movie (No, NOT the orgasm scene from *When Harry Met Sally*. Yes, this is informal, but you still have parents and clergy members here.) Or you or your friends might write an original piece. If you delegate this duty, make sure to see the play *before* the rehearsal dinner. What's funny to one person can be humiliating to another.

Give a Slide Show

Gather photos of the two of you, your family and members of your wedding party. Appoint someone from your wedding party to photo-research duty. She'll need to call all your friends and ask them to send photos. Get slides made of the photos and find quotes or quips and make a comment on each slide.

Share the Spotlight

Ask everyone to bring his or her favorite love- or marriage-related quote to the dinner. Take turns reading them aloud. You can collect the quotes afterward and bind them in a book. Send a copy to all the participants at the rehearsal dinner (after you return from your honeymoon, of course).

Give Gifts That Gab

The rehearsal dinner is the traditional time for you to give gifts to members of your wedding party. Rather than the standard photo album or silver-handled blush brush, make your gifts unique by making them speak. Here are some suggestions:

Sample Rehearsal Dinner Gifts

Bring on the Blankets

Winter wedding in Michigan? Give luxurious stadium blankets, with this fragment from a Native American marriage ceremony sewn in: *Now you will feel no cold, for each of you will be warmth to the other.* (COMFORT)

Say It with Stationery

Give elegant stationery sets in silver boxes, fun cardboard containers or plastic toolkits. Put these words by John Donne on the outside of the box: *More than kisses, letters mingle souls* (COURTSHIP). Include a personal letter from the two of you inside each box.

Engrave It

If you do go with a traditional silver present, add language to make yours more meaningful. You might give bridesmaids silver-plated vanity mirrors with this section from a poem by Tu Fu: *My beloved is mirrored on my heart.* (CONVICTION/DEVOTION)

Tap into Your Love of Travel

Globe-trotters? Give your attendants silver compasses with these words from "Simple Gifts": *. . . when we find ourselves in the place just right, it will be in the valley of love and delight.* (HAPPINESS, JOY AND LAUGHTER) Alternately, you might give an atlas, small globes or traveler's diaries (for recording impressions of their own trips) imprinted with these words.

Let Them Write

Poetic, introspective friends? Give your attendants leather-bound writing journals, with these words by Helen Hayes written on the inside:

> *. . . the story of a love*
> *is not important*
> *what is important*
> *is that one is capable of love.*
> *It is perhaps the only glimpse*
> *We are permitted of eternity.*
>
> (CONVICTION/DEVOTION)

Etch It

Give crystal goblets, etched with these lines (or include them on a note) from a Persian love poem: *I am a crystal goblet in my Love's hand. Look into my eyes if you don't believe me.* (CONVICTION/DEVOTION)

Make Menus That Speak

If you're having a formal, sit-down dinner complete with printed menus, consider including food for thought—in the form of a quote, quip or poem—along with the names of the dishes. Here's an example:

Sample Rehearsal Dinner Menu

Menu

APPETIZER:

ARUGULA SALAD WITH PEARS AND WALNUTS

"True love is the ripe fruit of a lifetime."
–ALPHONSE DE LAMARTINE

ENTRÉE (CHOICE OF):

Chicken

Mahi-mahi

Rack of lamb

"Love is a taste of Paradise."
–Shalom Aleichem

DESSERT:

Molten Valhrona Chocolate Cake with
Vanilla Bean Ice Cream

Wedding Cake

"He does not wait too long who waits for something good."
–Queen Christina of Sweden to Prince Karl Gustaff

Throughout the meal, local California white and red wine will be served.

"This life is a jar, and in it, union is the pure wine.
If we aren't together, of what use is the jar?"
–Persian love poem

Bachelor and Bachelorette Bashes

The old-style bachelor party (gyrating strippers, free-flowing booze), is quickly fading into memory. Today, friends are throwing more creative parties—everything from a white-water rafting weekend to a spa day. Whatever type of party you have, you can make it more memorable by including creative language. Having a picnic lunch by a lake? Take turns reading poems aloud. Think a language-based bash is a bit too, er, sweet for the guys? Make it a karaoke night and belt out those old, super-sappy make-out songs from the '80s.

Chapter 7

Your Ceremony

You're not the first couple to get married, but you are the first couple *exactly* like you to tie the knot. Use creative language throughout your ceremony to help express your feelings and the specifics of your relationship. You can incorporate quotes, quips, poetry and prose into your vows, and include readings and songs throughout your wedding ceremony.

∾ The Exchange of Vows ∾

While the fit of your new frock (or tails of your new tux) may seem like the most important part of your wedding, the vows are actually *the* main event—the one part of this whole affair that officially transforms you from pals to partners for life. Personalizing your vows is one of the best ways to assert the uniqueness of your union. How do you voice your deepest feelings artistically, without embarrassing you, your loved one, and the two hundred people assembled to watch? With help from the world's greatest wordsmiths, of course.

What's in a Ceremony?

Here's the basic rundown for a traditional wedding ceremony and some suggestions for adding a personal touch.

- Processional

- *(good spot for creative music)*

- Officiant's welcome and opening remarks

- *(good spot for personal thought from officiant, including a quote or piece of poetry)*

- Charge to the couple: Do you take this man to be your law-fully wedding husband, etc.

- *(good place for readings/music/poetry)*

- Vows

- Ring exchange

- *(good place for unity candle or other unity symbol/good spot for music or a short reading/good place for readings/music/poetry)*

- Pronouncement of marriage

- Seal It with a Kiss

- Officiant's closing remarks

- Recessional
  (good spot for creative music)

WOW! WHAT VOWS!
*Top Tips for Including Quotes
in Your Vows:*

Examine Tradition

Get a copy of the traditional wedding vows your officiant usually uses. If you're having a Christian or a civil ceremony, this will probably be a variation of the standard Protestant wedding vow spoken at many American weddings (and most Hollywood nuptials): "Do you promise to have and to hold, for better or for worse, for richer and for poorer, in sickness and in health, 'til death do you part?"

If you're having a Jewish wedding, your ceremony will include your wedding vows, a recitation of the Seven Blessings, and probably a reading of the Ketubah, or marriage contract. For an interfaith ceremony, take a look at both traditions—ask interfaith-friendly clergy and other interfaith couples you know for suggestions and resources.

Looking at the standard vows is a good way to begin thinking about the major marriage issues. Talk about what elements seem essential to both of you. Is it important to you to commit to loving each other even if your fortunes change, or is that so obvious as to seem irrelevant? Does this seem like the right time to address issues of health? Are you focused on staying together forever, or do you want your vows to relate more to how you feel today? The promises made in the standard vows relate to the big commitment issues. Many people feel that these are ideas they want to mention, whether or not they use the standard words.

Mull over the Meaning of Marriage

You may decide that while the standard vows address important issues, these ideas are not the glue that bond the two of you. Think about what ideas are critical to you, yet ignored by the standard vows. Discuss what

> **Two Religions,
> One Ceremony**
>
> For help planning a Christian/Jewish wedding, check out *Interfaith Wedding Ceremonies: Samples and Sources* (Dovetail Publishing). Call: 800-222-0070.

marriage means to the two of you and what, specifically, you want to promise to each other. Jot these ideas down.

Identify the Uniqueness of Your Union

Discuss the unique factors of your relationship. Are you two people from widely different cultures who have come together against all odds? Or maybe you grew up in the same town and have been dating off and on since third grade. Write down these distinguishing details.

Corral Your Favorite Quotes

Pick the quotes, quips and poetry from this book that you both love. Then set aside those that don't specifically relate to the key issues you've identified. These may be perfect pieces to print on your program or include as readings during the ceremony or reception, but they don't belong in your vows. Hang on to the ones that reiterate your ideas about marriage and/or about your marriage specifically.

Start Writing!

Write a first draft of your vows, building around the text you've selected. Feel free to chop up the selection, intersperse your own thoughts, and paraphrase parts that you feel you can say better yourselves. There is no copyright infringement when it comes to wedding vows. Do like TV newscasters do: Write short, simple, declarative sentences. They'll be easier for you to say and for others to understand. Don't worry if your vows sound cliché or mundane. This is just your first draft.

Personal Does *not* Mean Confessional

Don't talk about past difficulties in your relationship or within your families. Instead, focus on your positive future. If you use humor, stick to the big ideas. This is not the time to promise to make the morning coffee 'til death do you part. Remember, your vows are the most profound moment of the most important part of your wedding.

Read Aloud and Edit, Edit, Edit

Read your vows out loud. Rewrite or cut out any parts that sound clunky or repetitive. Continue fine-tuning each sentence until it says *exactly* what you mean. Then reread your edited versions aloud, changing any tongue twisters. Keep your final version under three minutes long.

Officiant Check!

Check with your officiant before writing your own vows. For a formal religious ceremony, you may not be able to stray too far from the traditional text. If you do go creative, your clergyman/woman will want to read your proposed vows to make sure they don't conflict with your religion.

Don't Leave Home Without It

Give a copy of your vows to your best man and maid of honor. And bring a copy with you on your wedding day. You *may* be a bit nervous and want them on hand.

Sample Personalized Vows

Anna and Ben spent the first five years of their relationship living on opposite coasts. After the wedding, they plan to live together in Baltimore, but their careers may take them in opposite directions again. They want their vows to reflect their unshakable unity, despite the potential physical distance.

BEN:

I, Ben, love and adore you, Anna.

I promise to always be here for you,

Though times be good or bad

Though we are near or far,

You are *flesh of my flesh,*

bone of my bone; I here, thou there, yet both one. (ANNE BRADSTREET, SOUL
    MATES/SYNERGY)

I will love, cherish and honor you,

'Til death do us part.

ANNA:

I, Anna, love and adore you, Ben.

I promise to always be here for you,

Though times be good or bad

Though we are near or far,

You are *flesh of my flesh,*

bone of my bone; I here, thou there, yet both one. (ANNE BRADSTREET, SOUL
    MATES/SYNERGY)

I will love, cherish, and honor you,

'Til death do us part.

❧

**Paul and Paquine met in Mexico City, where she lives. Her family is
Mexican and his is American. She has agreed to move to Houston to be
with him. They chose to quote the Bible to reflect the fact that they are
uniting two cultures. They will each read the vows in English and Spanish as a way to include both families.**

PAUL:

I, Paul, promise to love and respect you,

For better and for worse,

For richer and for poorer,
In sickness and in health
'Til death do us part.
I will always cherish your presence in my life,
Remembering the efforts you have made for me,
And striving always to merit your love.
Where you go I will go, and where you lodge I will lodge; your people shall
*   be my people, and your God my God.*

(RUTH, FOREVER LOVE)

PAQUINE:
I, Paquine, promise to love and respect you,
For better and for worse,
For richer and for poorer,
In sickness and in health
'Til death do us part.
I will always cherish your presence in my life,
Remembering the efforts you have made for me,
And striving always to merit your love.
Where you go I will go, and where you lodge I will lodge; your people shall
*   be my people, and your God my God.*

❧ Wedding Readings ❧

So what do you do with all those other great words that didn't make it into your vows? Include them as readings! Readings are a way to incorporate more of your personality into your ceremony—and to include your family and friends.

You can choose pieces to read yourselves, invite others to read, and/or ask your officiant to include a reading as part of his sermon or after you've said your vows. What makes a great reading? Read on.

Let Them Choose

If you can't figure out what your father, best friend or sister should read, ask them to make suggestions. You'll get them more involved and excited about their readings and save yourselves time. But maintain veto power—it's their reading, but it's still your wedding.

Officiant Check!

Check with your officiant before lining up readers; many officiants will want to clear any creative touches to make sure they don't conflict with the rules or traditions of the religion or house of worship.

RIGHT-ON READINGS!

Tips for Creating Great Readings

Cull Your Favorite Quotes

While your vows address the most fundamental issues of your relationship, ceremony readings can cover a broader range. A reading might relate to some element of your courtship, to your professions, to your passions, or to your ideas about family and/or marriage. A reading can be any form of poetry or prose that you feel will enhance the meaning of this moment. Look at the quotes, quips and prose pieces you love but didn't use in your vows. Which of these address other important ideas that you want to share? Go back through this book and see what other selections you like.

Combine and Cut

One of the best ways to make a reading personal is to combine elements from a few different sources. Maybe Shakespeare got it partly right, but Elvis really completed the thought. Combine them! And paraphrase any parts you can say better.

You also can wrap your favorite quotes around your own stories—an anecdote about how you met, a piece of advice you remember from your grandparents or anything else you want to share.

Contextualize

Whether you're taking a passage from a popular song or a piece from the Bible, let your listeners know what you're quoting and why. Briefly! Try to keep your introduction or explanation to one or two sentences.

Say you're quoting a poem by Rainer Maria Rilke. You might introduce it by saying, "This is a piece by Rainer Maria Rilke, a German poet who wrote the most moving poems about romantic longing that I've ever read. The first poem Bill ever sent me—by e-mail, I might mention—was by Rilke."

Include Others

While no one can say your vows but the two of you, anyone you choose can give a reading. Consider asking important people to read as a way to honor them and to include them in this moment. A reading by someone else can address love and marriage in general, or the relationship between the person giving it and the two of you.

If you have creative friends, consider asking them to write something to read, using any quotes or quips in this book to help. Ask your actor pals to act out a scene from your life or from literature. But make sure *you* hear it first. Even friends with the best intentions can unwittingly step on sensitive issues.

The "When and Where" of Readings

Generally, readings fall before the vows and after the ring exchange. But this is not a *rule*. Readings can go anywhere that works within the structure of your ceremony. As you craft your ceremony with your officiant, identify appropriate places for breaks.

Respect Your Readers

When asking others to read at your ceremony, remember that this is an honor, not a dare. If your ex-stepmother is uncomfortable reading in public, let her off the hook. Include her in your wedding in a way that she will enjoy instead.

Suzie and Brad grew up in the same town and have known each other since grade school. Though they went to colleges in different states, they both returned to their hometown to work, met once again and fell in love. Maybe "fell" is the wrong word. Neither ever fell in love with anyone else, and both always felt they'd somehow end up together. They wanted to address this unusual circumstance during their wedding.

SUZIE:

As many of you know, Brad and I had our first date on the playground in kindergarten. Many people ask us, "How can you marry your grade-school sweetheart? Haven't you changed since you were five? Haven't you dated other, different, more interesting people?" We have changed, certainly. And yes, we've both dated other people. But, in the end, as in the beginning, it was the two of us together.

I think Emily Brontë said it best in *Wuthering Heights*. We're paraphrasing slightly, but I think she'd understand: "*. . . you're more myself than I am. Whatever our souls are of, yours and mine are the same . . .*"

BRAD:

"*If all else perished and you remained, I should still continue to be, and if all else remained, and you were annihilated, the universe would turn to a might stranger . . . You're always, always in my mind; not as a pleasure to myself, but as my own being.*" (SOUL MATES/SYNERGY)

In this era of celebrity divorces and short-term marriage, Catherine always looked to her grandparents' steadfast relationship as a role

model. Given her closeness to her grandparents and her view of them as "sponsors" of her wedding, she asked them to give a reading about their view of long-term commitment. Grandma Ruth is a bit shy, so they decided that Grandpa Al would give the reading.

GRANDPA AL:

I am honored that Catherine and Mark asked me to say a few words tonight. Catherine has been coming over to our house since before she was born, and her grandma Ruth and I have always tried to show her how much richer love gets with age. I think this passage from Emerson's essay entitled "Love," says it better than I ever could:

"The world rolls; the circumstances vary every hour . . . The lovers' once flaming regard is sobered . . . and losing in violence what it gains in extent, it becomes a thorough good understanding."

I hear all you young people groaning. "Understanding! How Boring!" But Emerson continues:

"At last the lovers discover that all which at first drew them together—those once sacred features, that magical play of charms—had a prospective end, like the scaffolding by which the house was built, and the purification of the in-tellect and the heart, from year to year is the real marriage." (IT'S BETTER WHEN YOU'RE OLDER)

When I look at you, Catherine and Mark, I can already see how your love is making you both stronger and better. For your grandma Ruth and me, marriage has been a way to become better as individuals and as a team. This is what I wish, and know to be true, for the two of you.

~

Cynthia was in the library reading a book by her favorite poet, Walt Whitman, when she met Roberto. She feels like the meeting was fated, particularly because this piece expresses her feelings for him so well.

She always associates this poem with Roberto and decided to read a portion of it.

I do not offer the old smooth prizes
But offer rough new prizes,
These are the days that must happen to you:
You shall not heap up what is called riches,
You shall scatter with lavish hands all that you earn or achieve. . . .

Afoot and lighthearted, take to the open road,
Healthy, free, the world before you,
The long brown path before you, leading wherever you choose.
Say only to one another:
Comrade, I give you my hand!
I give you my love, more precious than money,
I give you myself before preaching or law:
Will you give me yourself?
Will you come travel with me?
Shall we stick by each other as long as we live?

(WALT WHITMAN, 'TIL DEATH DO YOU PART)

❧ Using Music ❧

Even if you have the world's all-time, most romantic relationship, silver screen stories have one up on you—a soundtrack. There's nothing like an orchestra bursting into music to intensify the emotional impact of any event. Make your ceremony more moving by creating your own sound-track—using music to escort you down the aisle and add pizzazz throughout your ceremony.

CREATE YOUR OWN SOUNDTRACK
You can include creative music in the traditional places:

- The Prelude: Music that fills the room before the ceremony begins, usually for about 30 minutes. This can be instrumental or vocal.

- The Processional: Music to which you march down the aisle. You can use different selections for the wedding party and the bride.

- The Recessional: Music that accompanies the new couple back up the aisle and out the door, followed by the wedding party.

- The Postlude: Music played as the guests leave the ceremony space.

. . . and throughout the ceremony

- Solos by friends and family: Can be performed after the mothers are seated, before or after the vows are spoken, or anywhere else that works within your ceremony.

- Group songs by the congregation: Can be performed in all the same places as a solo.

- Musical accompaniments: Can be used while lighting a unity candle, under readings and mediations.

MOVING MUSIC
Tips for a Tuneful Ceremony

Go Down the Aisle with Style

Why stroll down the aisle to "Here Comes the Bride" when there may be some other song that expresses your feelings better? Whether you hire a string trio or use recorded music, choose an instrumental version of whatever song sums up your feelings about your marriage.

Select Songs for Silent Prayers

Ask your ceremony musicians (or whoever is manning the boombox) to play something softly during silent prayers (or "moments of silence" in a civil ceremony). But listen to all potential selections first—even if your musician thinks an instrumental version of "Stairway to Heaven" is perfectly appropriate, you may not.

Ask Friends to Perform

Billy Idol your best man? Why ask him to give a reading, when he can sing your favorite song instead? Even if your friends aren't professional performers, asking them to sing (or strum or play the flute) is a great way to include them and to customize your ceremony. Start by considering the songs included in this book. Or ask your talented team to chose material themselves. But make sure to hear their choices before your wedding. Your dad may believe that ABBA is the world's best band, but your spouse-to-be may not.

Lead a Group Song

Consider asking everyone to join in on a group song. A singalong is a great way to get everyone involved. Consider printing the lyrics in your program to make sure everyone can participate.

Use Music While Lighting a Unity Candle

Consider a soft, instrumental accompaniment to the candle-lighting ceremony or underneath any other unity-symbol ceremony you include.

Include a Musical Tour of Your Ancestry

Honor your ancestors by giving a musical tribute. You can play music throughout your ceremony drawn from the various ethnic traditions that make up your families.

Officiant Check!

If you're having a religious ceremony, run your musical selections by your officiant first; some houses of worship have strict rules regarding what type of music can and cannot be played. While Protestant churches tend to accept both religious and secular music, some Catholic clergy may turn a deaf ear to requests for popular songs. A Reform or Conservative Jewish rabbi probably will be open to the inclusion of secular music, while an Orthodox one may require Hebrew or nothing.

Give Your Kids the Spotlight

If you're including (brave and talented) children (from a previous marriage or young relations), let them sing a featured song as a way to include them in the ceremony and help give them a sense of their own importance in your new marriage.

Classic Music Options

The Prelude
  "Air," from *Water Music*, Handel
  "Songs Without Words," Mendelssohn
  "Violin Concerto in A," Haydn

The Processional:
"Allemande," *G-Major Suite,* Pachelbel
"March," *Occasional Oratorio,* Handel
"Apotheosis," *Sleeping Beauty,* Tchaikovsky
"Wedding March," *The Marriage of Figaro,* Mozart

The Recessional:
"The Arrival of the Queen of Sheba," Handel
Brandenburg Concerto No. 1 in F (First Movement), J. S. Bach
"Pomp and Circumstance," March No. 4, Elgar
"Wedding March," from *A Midsummer Night's Dream,*
Mendelssohn

The Postlude:
"Drink This Wedding Toast," Big Mountain
"Chapel of Love," The Dixie Cups
"I Feel Good," James Brown
"ABC," The Jackson 5

Where to Get Great Music
Traditional processionals and recessionals:

7 Veils Record Company
1206 Richcreek Road
Austin, TX 78757
(512) 458-3539

Programs! Programs! Get Your Programs Here!

Even if your wedding is not the size of a rock concert, a ceremony program is a great way to let your friends and relatives know who's who and what's happening—particularly if you're having out-of-town guests or are joining different faiths or ethnic traditions. A program consists of:

- Your names, the date and the ceremony location

- The ceremony order

- Names of the members of your wedding party

- Names, photos and/or tributes to others you want to honor

- An explanation of religious and ethnic traditions that may be unfamiliar to your guests

- Lyrics, lines of poetry and blocks of prose being spoken during your ceremony

- Any other piece of poetry or prose you want to include

- A message from the two of you

❧ Making a Program ❧

Your program can be as simple or as ornate as you choose to make it. Some people include all the necessary info on an 8 ½" × 11" piece of paper, printed out on a home computer and folded in halfs or in thirds. Use an elegant typeface, unique paper and scanned or computer-generated art to dress it up without breaking the bank.

If you have a bigger budget, you might want a several-page program professionally printed and bound. (You can order your program from the stationery store when you order invitations and thank-you notes.) Most copy shops also can do professional-quality printing and binding. Ask around about options and expense.

Whether you do desktop publishing or hire a professional printer, consider matching your program to the style and theme of your wedding. For a Victorian affair, you might create a fancy scroll printed in italic type and tied with a silk ribbon. For a literary wedding, you could write a mini-book to tell the tale of your union, using quotes to start each "chapter." For a Valentine's Day nuptial, make your program resemble an old-fashioned, Valentine's card. Your creativity is your only limit.

POETIC PROGRAMS
Top Tips for Using Quotes in Your Program

Print Quotes from Your Ceremony

Print any pieces of poetry or prose you plan to say (or have said) during your ceremony. While your guests will hear them during the ceremony, a printout lets them really absorb the words.

Include Quotes, Readings and Poems That Didn't Make the Ceremony

Don't forget those great pieces that landed on the cutting-room floor when you wrote your vows and chose your readings. Since you've found so many pieces of powerful prose and poetry that express your feelings about marriage, your program is the perfect place to print up these words and sentiments for your guests to take home.

Appoint a Program Passer

Ask a relative or friend to pass out programs as guests enter the ceremony space. This is a good way to include another person in your wedding—a young cousin or a good friend who is not part of the bridal party

Honor Thy Ancestors

Include a poem or quote as an homage to a departed relative or friend. It might be the lyrics to your grandfather's favorite song, a quote by a great statesman your great-uncle admired or a piece of writing that simply reminds you of someone you've loved.

Interview Your Wedding Party

Ask members of your wedding party and/or your parents or other relatives to choose their favorite quotes about love and marriage. Print their selections in your program following their names and their relationship to you.

Sample Programs

Amy and Richard met on a nature expedition in Bermuda. Big outdoor buffs, they're having an eco-wedding (outdoors, saplings as party favors, birdseed instead of rice, donating any leftover food to a local homeless shelter). They are creating a program (printed on recycled paper) that relates to their shared passion for the planet.

Program Cover:

Field Guide to Amy and Richard's Wedding

Saturday, June 21, 2002
Prospect Park, Brooklyn, New York

The fountains mingle with the river,
And the rivers with the ocean;
The winds of heaven mix forever,
With a sweet emotion;
Nothing in the world is single;
All things by a law divine
In one another's being mingle;
Why not I with thine?
—Percy Bysshe Shelley*

---

*(SOUL MATES/SYNERGY)

(Inside left-hand page)

Welcome to the wedding of Amy Smith and Richard Wright.
As many of you know, Amy and Richard met during a nature
expedition in Bermuda, and feel that their love was a gift from
Mother Nature. Please sit back and enjoy their wedding—a
"natural expedition" of the most important kind.

ORDER OF EVENTS:
Sermon: Reverend Arthur Dimsdale
Reading of Poem of R. W. Raymond by Michelle Smith
Vows
Exchange of Rings
Lighting of Unity Candle
Pronouncement of Marriage and Closing
Recessional

(Inside right-hand page)

Then blend they, like green leaves with golden flowers,
Somewhere there waiteth in this world of ours
For one lone soul, another lonely soul.
Each choosing each through all the weary hours . . .
—EDWIN ARNOLD, (SOUL MATES/SYNERGY)

I am the sky. You are the earth. We are the earth and sky, united.

—Hindu wedding ceremony*
(Read by the bride and groom during the Unity Candle ceremony)

(Back page)
Bountiful thanks to our parents for helping with the wedding and to all
of you for being here today to share it

---

*(SOUL MATES/SYNERGY)

⟡

Emma Bovary is an architect and Vincent Spario is an industrial engineer. They met on a job site, became friends, fell in love, and eventually quit their jobs to open up an architectural firm together. They view their relationship as a union of souls and life paths, and though their fledgling company is still in the red, they wanted their ceremony to reflect their deep joy at having found each other and their sense of ultimate luck at being together.

Cover:
Emma Bovary and Vincent Spario
September 7
Museum of Fine Arts Sculpture Garden
Houston, TX

(Inside left-hand page)
Marriage is the fusion of two hearts, the union of two lives—the coming together of two tributaries.
—Peter Marshall*

ORDER OF CEREMONY
Processional
Justice of the Peace Ann Holmes Delivers an Introduction
The Bride and Groom Say Their Vows
The Bride and Groom Exchange Rings
Justice of the Peace Holmes Makes the Pronouncement of Marriage
Closing Remarks
Recessional

THE WEDDING PARTY:

Maid of Honor: Valeri Parker
(the bride's best friend from high school)

———————
*(SOUL MATES/SYNERGY)

Bridesmaids: Ann Cerry, Sandy Stevens,
Sue Sugar, Debbi Chekov

Best Man: Max Spario (the groom's brother)

Groomsmen: Brian Dickenson, David King,
George Panderas, Adam Mark

Honor Couple: Amanda Sparks and Aaron Chester (Emma and
Vincent view these two as their romantic role model and steadfast
supportive team)

(Inside right-hand page)

Where they create dreams,
There were not enough for both of us,
So we saw the same one . . .
—Anna Akhmatova, from "Instead of an Afterword"*
(Read by Justice of the Peace Ann Holmes)

(Back page)
For thy sweet love remember'd such wealth brings,
That then I scorn to change my state with kings.

—William Shakespeare, Sonnet XXIX**

---

*(SOUL MATES/SYNERGY)
**(PARTNERSHIP, FRIENDSHIP AND COMPANIONSHIP)

Chapter 8

Your Reception

You have cocktails, cake and fifty of your closest friends cutting up the dance floor. But your reception isn't only dinner and dancing—it's also a continued celebration of your commitment and love. Incorporating creative language is a great way to personalize this party, include others in the moment and make it more than just another Saturday night.

The most obvious place to use quotes is during the toasts—both those you give and those you receive. But there are dozens of other ways to add your own voice by incorporating the words of others.

✌ Time for Toasting ✌

You *can* give great, personal yet entertaining toasts—even if you weren't the star of your high school debate team and never took a toast-masters course. Find the quote, lyric or passage that says exactly what you feel, and build your stellar speech around that.

TERRIFIC TOASTS

Top Tips for Using Quotes in Your Toasts

Be Specific about the Toastee

Write down the name of the person you're toasting and his or her link to you. Think about your relationship and jot down about half a dozen of your best memories and shared moments. These might be anecdotes about how you met, some profound experience you shared or an event when this person really made a difference in your life. Pick one or two examples to build your toast around. A toast that focuses on a personal, specific instance of how someone impacted you is always stronger and more interesting than one that merely states, "Well, gee, Kathy is really great and nice and smart." You listeners want to know *why* she's great and *how,* exactly.

Consider This Toast an Extension of Your Ceremony

If you don't have a specific story to tell, think about the ideas you discussed and dismissed when writing your vows. You might be able to recast one of these as part of your toast. Remember, this *is* a party. Did something hilarious happen that you couldn't discuss during the solemnity of the ceremony? Now might be the time to tell. If you tell a funny anecdote, end it on a serious note by explaining how this story highlights an important trait of the toastee.

Look to the Wedding Itself for Ideas

Think about the wedding process, too. How has it deepened your conviction that you chose the right spouse, best friend, officiant, wedding hall? You might choose to build your toast around something you learned during this whole process.

Pull Quotes That Express It Best

Read through the quotes in this book, pulling the ones that relate to the anecdote, idea or experience you want to mention in your toast.

Start Writing

Write a first draft of your toast, incorporating the ideas and quotes you've noted. You can start your toast with a quote, drop it in the middle or tack it on the end. Feel free to use more than one quote, trim the selection and/or paraphrase however you like.

Don't worry if your first draft is ten pages long and as boring as a slide show about rocks. First, get all your ideas down. Then spend at least as much time editing your thoughts into your official first draft.

If you plan to speak off-the-cuff (rather than reading something written), spend some time identifying and organizing the ideas you want to address. Jot down these themes on index cards so that you can speak extemporaneously, yet eloquently. You may want to completely write out the text you're going to quote, however, just in case you're overcome by nerves (or champagne).

Read (or Speak) Aloud and Edit. Edit. Edit

Make sure you can read your toast comfortably. Rewrite any sentences that trip you up, sound dull, redundant, embarrassing or unnecessary. The art of good writing is rewriting. Time your toast and try to keep it under three minutes. When you give your toast, make sure to pause for laughter; they can't hear you when they're laughing.

Don't Leave Home Without It

Whether you write out the whole toast, or just note key words on index cards, bring a cheat sheet just in case.

Toasting Traditions—Who Speaks When

• The best man starts by toasting the bride and groom—after cocktails have been served or during dinner.

• The groom toasts the best man, his bride, both sets of parents and anyone else he would like to acknowledge.

• The bride toasts her new husband, all the assembled parents and any friends or relatives.

• Anyone who desires to speak does. If your time is limited but your friends are loquacious, put your wedding coordinator or band leader on overtime alert. Ask him to step in and stop the toasting after a certain amount of time to avoid turning your wedding into open-mike night.

Toasting Etiquette

Generally, the person giving the toast stands and delivers from wherever he is (unless there is a bandleader conducting the event and calling toasters up to the front of the room). Everyone else remains seated (even the toastee—keep your seat when being toasted).

Alternately (or in addition), you could do an informal round of toasting with your closest friends. Gather together during the cocktails or sometime after dinner and ask everyone to take turns saying something impromptu and heartfelt.

How to Get Good Toast

Notify people ahead of time if you want them to give a toast and offer direction: "No, do *not* discuss all my old girlfriends. Why don't you explain how you were the one who set us up instead?"

Remember—asking someone to give a toast should be an honor. If your best man would rather swim naked in an icy pond than speak in public, ask the maid of honor to lead the toasting instead. Happiness and comfort preside over tradition.

Sample Best Man's Toast

Bill Schwartz asked his brother Zachary to be his best man. Zachary is seventeen years older than Bill and has had the dual role of sibling/ older uncle–type for their whole lives.

ZACHARY:

"I've known Bill since before he was born. While other high school juniors were taking their girls to lovers' lane, I would stay home and baby-sit for infant Bill. Our parents were amazed that I was so responsible, so willing to stay home on a Saturday night with a baby, never showing signs of secretly wanting to squash him with a pillow. But what the folks did not know is that a baby brother is a chick magnet. Girls love to hang out with guys with babies! It's the ultimate aphrodisiac. So thank you, Bill, and thank you, Mom and Dad, for providing me with such a successful, and love-filled high school career.

"Bill has been a blessing in my life in other ways, too. It's amazing how grounding a baby brother can be, how much his growth forced me to put my own ambition in perspective and to remember the value of family and other people you love. Although I do remember thinking, as he got to college, 'This kid is so smart, he's going to get out of med school before I do.' Had that been the case, I might have squashed him with a pillow.

"Now, I look at you and I can't believe you're getting married. I'm so proud of you, for all that you've done, and for choosing such a wonderful woman to share your life. Sandra, I haven't known you for all my life . . . but it's been long enough for me to see that you are a kind, caring, devoted woman, as smart as Bill, and possibly as ambitious. I feel fortunate to have you as part of my family, and I look forward to a lifetime getting to know you better.

"You know, as they say, *"The value of marriage is not that adults produce children, but that children produce adults."* (PETER DE VRIES, MATURITY) I look at Bill and Sandra today and I see that Bill is not my baby brother any longer. You're two adults on your own, with the brightest future ahead of you. To Bill and Sandra."

Sample Groom's Toast

BILL:

"Thank you, Zachary. My brother Zachary, as most of you know, is seventeen years older than I am. While that age spread made me miss out on the thrill of sibling rivalry my friends always talked about, it also gave me something most kids did not have—a second father, or a very lenient uncle. I could tell Zachary anything and get real advice without getting sent to my room without dinner. Zach mentions my career success and I have to credit that, and my understanding that no matter how successful one becomes, family and friends are more important, not only to my parents but also to the example of my brother Zach. Here's to you, Zach.

"And to my parents, for providing me with Zach and for supporting me emotionally and financially on what seemed, at times, to all of us, like an endless journey toward adulthood and success.

"Speaking of success, I quote Winston Churchill, *'My most brilliant achievement was my ability to persuade my wife to marry me.'* (SUCCESS) Many late nights during med school, I'd get up from my books, go pour another cup of coffee, see my reflection in the old rusty coffeepot and think, 'I am the world's biggest loser. No one's ever going to marry me.' But then I met Sandra.

And it was like someone turned the lights on, like everything was suddenly brighter and airier and better. (HAPPINESS, JOY AND LAUGHTER)

"Mr. and Mrs. Wiley, thank you for raising your beautiful, wonderful daughter, and for thinking I'm good enough for her. Please know that you're not losing a daughter, you're gaining a family doctor.

"I'd also like to thank all of my friends for being here tonight and for putting up with me until now. I'd like to thank my family, and all of you who traveled across the country to be here to support Sandra and me on this day."

Sample Bride's Toast

"Bill, you have not only made things brighter, you have put them in sharper focus. As Ginger Rogers, who said, 'When two people love each other, they don't look at each other, they look in the same direction.' (PARTNERSHIP, FRIEND-SHIP AND COMPANIONSHIP) I think this is what made me fall in love with Bill in the first place. Right away, I felt that we were looking at the world through the same lens. That we understood each other and could face life's challenges and joys together. As many of you know, I did a bit of dating before meeting Bill. And from the moment I met Bill, I knew that he was the person I wanted to spend my life with, the one man who I would want on my side, to move forward with me. Here's to Bill, my new husband. I love you and look forward to living my life with you.

"And I'd like to thank Mr. and Mrs. Schwartz, and Zachary, apparently, for raising such a wonderful person. Bill is the love of my life, and I know he will help me live my life better and better. To quote Goethe, *"We are shaped and fashioned by what we love."* (JOHANN WOLFGANG VON GOETHE, GROWTH) There's no one I would trust to shape and fashion me more.

"I also want to thank my own parents, for showing me what I wanted in marriage. Growing up with parents so obviously in love taught me to wait for the right man, to only marry someone with whom I could share that kind of happiness. I certainly waited. And I continue to look toward the two of you as role models for the kind of marriage Bill and I hope to create.

"I'd like to thank my relatives for coming here tonight. And lastly, my friends—you know who you are—who listened to me go on and on . . . and on . . . about Bill during the nearly two years of our dating. I know it must have seemed interminable, and I'm sure that you are almost as happy as I am to see me standing here today."

Other Ways to Use Words of Love

There's more to your reception than standing around talking. Spread the love around—literally.

Guest Book

If you're having a formal guest book, write one of your favorite quotes on the opening page. Or top each page with words that say "wedding" to you. Guests can sign under a category that inspires them. Pull quotes from the front of this book, looking specifically under the "Love," "Marriage Itself" and "Wives" sections. Your quotes might hint at topics guests can address, such as:

No cord nor cable can so forcibly draw, or hold so fast, as love can do with a twined thread. (ROBERT BURTON, LOVE); *Those who are married live happily ever after the wedding day if they persevere in the real adventure, which is the royal task of creating each other and creating a more loving world.* (ARCHBISHOP OF CANTERBURY, MARRIAGE ITSELF); *An ideal wife is any woman who has an ideal husband.* (BOOTH TARKINGTON, WIVES).

Table Cards

Your guests arrive at the Superdome—which you've rented for this affair—and look among the rows of table cards for their names and table numbers. Since it's your wedding, each table card also has a quote about love under the number.

You could vary the quotes—and use them as conversation starters—by giving each guest at a table a different one. Alternately, you might "number" your tables by quotes. Each table is topped by one quote sitting on a stand in the center; each guest at that table has the same quote on his card. Guests find their tables by looking for the matching quotes.

Your table card quotes might relate to the pending event (sitting down): *When the one man loves the one woman and the one woman loves the one man, the very angels desert heaven and come and sit in that house and sing for joy.* (BRAHMA SUTRA, HAPPINESS, JOY AND LAUGHTER). Or they might point toward the great conversations everyone (hopefully) will be having during dinner: *A happy marriage is a long conversation that always seems too short* (ANDRÉ MAUROIS, HAPPINESS, JOY AND LAUGHTER). Look through the front of this book for quotes that seem meal-appropriate to you.

Table Toppers

Once your guests make their way to the tables, in addition to the hand-made candles topping the cloth and the fabulous floral centerpieces, they'll find—you guessed it—more romantic language. You can display tabletop quotes in various ways:

• Print them out on a computer and scatter among the dishes, flatware, glasses, etc.

• Write them with a silver pen on fancy doilies set under the butter dish, salt shakers, etc. Or write this line by Charles Dickens on cards at each plate: *How glad we shall be, that we have somebody we are fond of always, to talk to and sit with.* (COMFORT)

• Scatter candy conversation hearts (the kind available at Valentine's Day) on the tables. Or get larger ones made at a local candy shop, decorated with quotes you choose, such as: *We are word and meaning united.* (HINDU MARRIAGE RITUAL, SOUL MATES/ SYNERGY); and *No one worth possessing can be quite possessed.* (SARA TEASDALE, SURPRISE)

Wedding Favors

Why give the usual sugar-coated almonds when you can give something that says "love" best? Here are some suggestions for wedding favors that say what you mean—literally:

• Give pocket-sized books of poetry (available at any big chain bookstore). Or make minibooks yourselves, using your favorite twenty quotes. Print them out on your computer and get them bound at a copy shop.

• Give magnetic poetry sets to let people make their own love poems on the spot.

• Maybe you met just six months ago and couldn't wait another moment to tie the knot. Give guests coffee mugs imprinted with these words (from *When Harry Met Sally*): *When you realize you want to spend the rest of your life with somebody, you want the rest of your life to start as soon as possible.* (CONVICTION/DEVOTION)

• Having a sock hop wedding? Give guests cushy socks to slip into, with these words from William Butler Yeats embroidered or imprinted on them. (Put the first line on one sock and the second on the other). *I have spread my dreams under your feet; Tread softly because you tread on my dreams.* (CONVICTION/DEVOTION)

• Put something whimsical in front of each place setting, such as a small, children's kaleidoscope, a crystal in a velvet bag, a small globe, or a snow globe with a scene from your hometown. Tie with a card that says this line by Nikki Giovanni: *We love because it's the only true adventure.* (LOVE)

• Put an invisible pen-and-ink kit (kids' sets are available in any toy store) in front of each place, with a card that says: *To love someone is to see a miracle invisible to others* (FRANÇOIS MAURIAC, CONVICTION/ DEVOTION).

Singalong

Maybe you're having a country hoedown style wedding. Print lyrics to your favorite song and invite everyone to sing along.

Dessert

Order customized fortune cookies and stuff them with your favorite quotes. You might chose "fortunes" such as these: *Love cures people, both the ones who give it and the ones who receive it.* (DR. KARL MENNINGER, LOVE IN A TIME OF SICKNESS); *If it is your time, love will track you down like a cruise missile* (LYNDA BARRY, LOVE); and *If you would be loved, love and be lovable* (BENJAMIN FRANKLIN, LOVE).

Decorations

Use language to make unique decorative flourishes. You might create a giant arch for your guests to walk under on the way to the reception or to pose in front of for photos. Decorate it with flowers and your favorite quote. If it's an evening wedding under the stars, for example, you might write this line from a Persian love poem: *Tonight is a night of union and also of scattering of the stars* (WEDDING DAY) over the arch. Look through the front of this book for words that relate to the two of you and your wedding.

Order oversized ribbons printed with wedding words. (Check with a company that does personalized corporate and/or social monogramming, printing and engraving.) Tie them to the back of chairs, run them through the railing on a staircase, bind bunches of flowers or balloons with them, or use them to tie back curtains.

Write words of love directly on balloons, spray them in artificial snow on windows or hang them with fishing line from the ceiling.

Chapter 9

Second Wedding or Vow Renewal

❧ Remarriage ❧

Many people who have wed before find themselves freer to create the wedding of *their* dreams (rather than that of their family or friends) the second time around. When remarrying, you're older, wiser, more certain about what you want from life and from marriage.

There are no special rules about the size or scope of a second wedding. It can be as large and formal or as small and intimate as you want. The most important thing is to create a wedding that could only be for the two of you. How? By incorporating poetry and prose into the ceremony and reception, of course.

Kids Will Be Kids

Even if they don't say vows, your children can play a part in your wedding. They can do anything from passing out programs or serving as flower children, to giving readings, lighting a "family candle," or acting as the maid of honor or best man. But don't expect them to do more than they could do on any ordinary Saturday afternoon. Including them should make them feel special, not embarrassed or overburdened.

Readings for Children

If your children will be giving a reading, help them select something from a favorite book of theirs. Many children's books, such as *Winnie the Pooh, Charlotte's Web* or *The Little Prince,* have passages relating to wedding-appropriate topics, such as trust, loyalty and friendship. The familiarity of the book should help children feel more comfortable.

SECOND CEREMONIES
Top Tips to Personalize with Poetry and Prose

Write Your Own Vows

This is the time to write your own vows to express exactly what this marriage means to you, using quotes that help you express it. Look at Chapter 7 for tips on vow writing. While your vows shouldn't dwell on negative aspects of your previous marriage, they can mention how the knowledge you've gained from the past will strengthen your commitment to this new marriage.

Have Your Children Say "Vows"

If you have kids from a previous marriage, consider including them in the ceremony by writing "family vows." After the two of you say your vows, your officiant can ask your kids to accept their new siblings as stepsiblings or to accept your new spouse as a stepparent.

Give Kids a Physical Symbol of Unity

Present your children with a locket, a "family medallion" (three interlocking circles on a chain, for example) or a bracelet to symbolize their role in your new union. Engrave the item with a quote about the nature of family, unity or love. Before ordering anything, however, make sure your spouse-to-be, your children and your ex-spouse are comfortable with this gesture.

Include Readings

As with a first wedding, readings are one of the best ways to include other people in your ceremony. You may ask your children, friends who stood by you through tough times, new friends and even ex in-laws (depending on how close you are). Turn to Chapter 7 for tips on choosing and including ceremony readings.

Processional/Recessional

Make your ceremony unique by using your favorite songs throughout. You can select music with personal resonance to guide you down the aisle, play softly under silent meditations, be sung vigorously as a solo by a talented friend or by the entire congregation and/or to accompany you back up the aisle for the recessional. Turn to Chapter 7 for tips on choosing ceremony music.

A Second for One?

If it's the second marriage for one of you but the first for the other, recognize that you may have different attitudes toward the wedding itself. Second-time partner: Do *not* make comments like, "Last time we used this florist . . ." or "Who cares about engraved matchbooks? It's just a wedding." Be considerate of your soon-to-be-spouse and the newness of this event. First-time partner: Do *not* obsess about the fact that one of you has done this before. Don't ask about the first wedding. Don't look through old wedding photo albums. Keep your mind focused on *your* event. And both of you remember: This is just the wedding. No matter how differently you feel about the ceremony and reception, your views about marriage are what will hold you together.

Light a Unity Candle

A unity candle is a symbol of two families or two partners joining together as one. Look for quotes to read during the candle lighting, paying particular attention to those listed under the sections entitled Partnership, Friendship and Companionship; Soul Mates/Synergy; and Hardship.

Don't Forget a Program!

A second wedding is a first-rate time to use a ceremony program, both as a way to include quotes that express your feelings best and to honor important people in your lives. Turn to Chapter 7 for help creating a perfect program.

Sample Second Ceremony Vows
(With Children)

Joy Hope and Jim Green have two children each from previous marriages—ages seven through twelve. They both have full custody of their kids and will be creating a *Brady Bunch*–style blended family through their marriage. Because of the importance of their children in their new lives, they chose to have the kids stand up with them throughout the ceremony and say vows of their own, after the official wedding vows.

OFFICIANT (TO JIM)

Repeat after me:

I, Jim, take you, Joy, to be my wife, my friend, and my love: to share my life with you. I will strive to make our marriage a *partnership in which each inspires the other, and brings fruition to both.* (MILLICENT CAREY MCINTOSH) I promise to support you in all of your dreams and to help you be all that you aspire to be. I will stand by you, when our lives are filled with triumph and when times are tough. I will trust and honor you. I will act as a parent to your children and as a buoy, support and ballast to you.

OFFICIANT (TO JOY)

Repeat after me:

I, Joy, do take you, Jim, to be my husband, my friend, my partner and my love: to share my life with you. I will strive to make our marriage a *partnership in which each inspires the other, and brings fruition to both.* I promise to support you in all of your dreams and to help you be all that you aspire to be. I will stand by you, when our lives are filled with triumph and when times are tough. I will trust and honor you. I will act as a parent to your children and as a buoy, support and ballast to you.

OFFICIANT (TO JOY'S CHILDREN)

Michelle and Amber, do you accept Keith and Matthew as your stepbrothers?

(Michelle and Amber say, "I do.")

OFFICIANT (TO JIM'S CHILDREN)

And Keith and Matthew, do you accept Michelle and Amber as your stepsisters?

(Keith and Matthew say, "I do.")

Sample Second Ceremony Vows
(Without Children)

Phil and Margaret came into this marriage with some difficulty. They were both still going through divorces when they met. Though their friends and family advised them to wait until their divorces were finalized, spend a year being single, and *then* see if their interest in each other persisted, their passion for each other made this moderation impossible. They wanted their vows to acknowledge the difficulties of the past and their optimistic outlook for the future.

PHIL:

I take you, Margaret, to be my wife, friend and support from this day forward,
To join with you and to share all that I have, all that I am, and all that I will be.
I'll give you the future if you'll forgive me my past. (KENNY ROGERS, COMPROMISE)
And I will strive to make our future brighter than any star.

MARGARET:

I take you, Phil, to be my husband, friend and support from this day forward,
To join with you and to share all that I have, all that I am and all that I will be.
I'll give you the future if you'll forgive me my past.
And I will strive to make our future brighter than any star.

Sample Second Wedding Readings

**One of Phil and Margaret's friends viewed their compulsion toward
each other as a sign of the kind of passion you usually only read about
in books. Margaret's best friend, Amelia, chose to read this poem to
express the intensity of their love.**

Two such as you, with
Such a master speed
Cannot be parted
Nor be swept away
From one another
Once you are agreed

That life is only
life forevermore
Together
wing to wing
and oar to oar.

ROBERT FROST, (SOUL MATES/SYNERGY)

Thelma had been married to an untrustworthy, nonsupportive man for five years. She finally ended that marriage and met David two years later. She feels David is the first man who really supports, loves and protects her. This is David's first marriage. During pre-marriage counseling with the priest, he confessed that he had almost given up on the idea of ever getting married, until he met Thelma. The priest chose to give this reading as part of his address because he felt it helped sum up their feelings about meeting each other.

Now you will feel no rain,
For each of you will be shelter for the other.

Now you will feel no cold,
For each of you will be warmth to the other.

Now you will feel no loneliness.

Now you are two persons.
But, there is only one life before you.

Go now to your dwelling to enter
Into the days of your life together.

And may your days be good,
And long upon the earth.

(NATIVE AMERICAN MARRIAGE CEREMONY, COMFORT)

SECOND RECEPTIONS

As with the ceremony, many people marrying for the second time feel far freer to throw the post-nup party of their dreams. A second reception can include all of the same elements as a first wedding reception, or it can take a completely new turn. See Chapter 8 for tips on using quotes, quips, poetry and prose to make this party personal.

Vow Renewals/ Reaffirmation

A vow renewal ceremony is an intrinsically personal event. Because it's an emotional, rather than a legal act, your own taste is your only limit on creative expression. You can renew your vows any time you want—one week after your first wedding or fifty years later. The goal is to repledge your commitment to each other and to emphasize what the two of you have built together. You can use creative language when writing formal vows, when giving a less formal address or reading and throughout the party.

CREATIVE REAFFIRMATION

Top Tips for Including Quotes
When Writing a Vow Renewal

Review Your Original Vows

You may want to restate your original vows in their entirety, adapted to fit your current circumstances (I promised and continue to promise to honor . . .), or choose to use only those sections that have taken on increased resonance over time.

Many religions have standardized reaffirmation vows, which you may want to consider including as well. Check with your clergyman, rabbi or the officiant from your original wedding.

Ask Yourselves "Why?"

Think about why you want to renew your vows and what this ceremony means to you. Did you elope the first time and now want a huge affair to share with all the people you love? Are you renewing your vows to show your children and grandchildren the growth of love over time? Have you recently come out of a rough period in your relationship and are now reaffirming your commitment? Or do you crave a huge party to celebrate the fact that you've made it this far together? Write down these reasons.

Who Will Officiate?

Since this is not a legal act, anyone can oversee your reaffirmation ceremony—a judge, family member, friend or mentor. If you're planning to do it in a church or synagogue, however, you will probably be required to have a clergy member sanction your vows.

Reflect on the Growth of Your Relationship

Use this opportunity to reflect on any difficulties you've overcome and victories you've achieved together. Jot these ideas down.

Take Another Look at Each Other

Think about the qualities of your spouse you love the most—patience, a sense of humor, the ability to constantly surprise you, etc. Write down these things, too.

Take a Look at Those Who Have Helped

If you've been together for twenty-five years, chances are, a handful of other people have contributed to the strength and development of your marriage. Use this opportunity to acknowledge their help and support. You might want to thank your children, your parents, other relatives, your friends, spiritual leaders, etc.

Find Quotes That Say It Best

Look through the quotes in this book to see which ones best state your feelings about your marriage and your reasons for reaffirming it. Look particularly at the sections Conviction/Devotion, Growth, Forever Love and It's Better When You're Older.

Start Writing

Write your first draft, combining your original vows, the quotes you've chosen and any words of your own. You may choose to repeat each other's vows or to write two different sets to express what your marriage means to each of you individually.

Read Aloud and Edit, Edit, Edit

Listen to how your vows sound out loud. Rewrite any phrases that seem awkward or difficult to say. Continue editing until you're comfortable with every sentence and feel the vows express exactly what you mean.

Don't Leave Home Without It

Just because you're older and wiser, doesn't mean you're exempt from nerve-induced forgetfulness. Bring a copy of your vows with you just in case.

Sample Vowal Renewals

Sarah and John are reaffirming their vows after thirty years of marriage. They wanted to repeat their original vows and recite two poems that express for them the continued strength and style of their love.

OFFICIANT:
Do you, John, take Sarah to be your wife? To have and to hold, for better and for worse, in sickness and in health, from this day forward?

JOHN:
I do and I did.
Sarah,
How much do I love thee?
Go ask the deep sea
How many rare gems
In its coral caves be,
Or ask the broad billows,
That ceaselessly roar
How many bright sands
So they kiss on the shore?
(MARY ASHLEY TOWNSEND, CONVICTION/DEVOTION)

OFFICIANT:
Do you, Sarah, take John to be your husband? To have and to hold, for better and for worse, in sickness and in health, from this day forward?

SARAH:
I do and I did.

JOHN,

The memories of long love
Gather like drifting snow,
Poignant as the mandarin ducks,
Who float side by side in sleep.

Falling from the ridge
Of high Tsukuba
The Minano River
At last gathers itself,
Like my love, into
A deep, still pool.

(KENNETH REXROTH, FOREVER LOVE)

Valerie and Glen have been married for fifteen years, but the past two have been very trying. Glen was having difficulty in his career and began feeling pessimistic about the world in general. He took some of his unhappiness out on Valerie. Valerie began to feel that Glen did not value her or their marriage. They separated for six months, talked to a marriage counselor, and reevaluated their relationship. Now, they are coming back into the marriage with renewed love and enthusiasm. They are renewing their vows to affirm their recommitment.

VALERIE:

I promise you, the man I have loved so long, to continue to love you with all my heart, all my soul and all my might.

I will strive to be more understanding of the ways in which we are different and to support the development of you, in any way I can.

I will let go of any past resentments and look toward the future with an open mind and an open heart.

I will stand by you in this next phase of life, whatever it may bring.

Love seems the swiftest, but it is the slowest of all growths. (MARK TWAIN, IT'S BET-
TER WHEN YOU'RE OLDER)

I promise to continue nurturing our love so that, as we grow older, the strength
of our commitment will grow, too.

GLEN:

I promise you, the woman I have loved so long, to continue to love you with all
my heart, all my soul and all my might.

I will be more open emotionally and let you know, daily, how much your presence has enriched my life.

I will strive to be more optimistic, braver, stronger and more noble.

I know that *marriage must exemplify friendship's highest ideal,* (MARGARET E.
SANGER, PARTNERSHIP, FRIENDSHIP AND COMPANIONSHIP) and I will strive to be the
true friend you have always been to me.

I look to you as a *teacher, tender comrade, wife,*

A fellow-farer true through life. (ROBERT LOUIS STEVENSON, PARTNERSHIP, FRIENDSHIP
AND COMPANIONSHIP)

I promise to continue nurturing our love so that, as we grow older, the strength
of our commitment will grow, too.

∾ Reaffirmation Readings ∾

A reading is another way to share your feelings with those assembled
and to give others a chance to voice their sentiments. You can read a selection in its entirety or create a reading of your own by combining elements
of several selections. Turn to Chapter 7 for help selecting and creating readings.

Sample Vow Renewal Readings

Anna Quixley and Hector Smith have been married for twenty years. After Hector's recent retirement, they sold their house in Wisconsin and moved to a new condo in Florida. They feel like they are entering "stage two" of their married life and wanted a vow renewal ceremony to help them officially usher in their new existence together.

HECTOR:

Your wedding-ring wears thin, dear wife; ah, summers not a few,
    Since I put it on your finger first, have passed o'er me and you;
And, love, what changes we have seen—what cares and pleasures, too,—
Since you became my own dear wife, when this old ring was new!
The past is dear, its sweetness still our memories treasure yet;
The griefs we've borne, together borne, we would not now forget.
Whatever, wife, the future brings, heart unto heart still true,
We'll share as we have shared all else since this old ring was new.

(WILLIAM COX BENNETT, FOREVER LOVE)

ANNA:

Grow old along with me!
The best is yet to be.
The last of life, for which the first was made.
Our times are in His hand.
Who saith, A whole I planned,
Youth shows but half. Trust God, see all, nor be afraid!

(ROBERT BROWNING, FOREVER LOVE)

∽

The children of Ruth and Brian Dickenson wanted to honor their parents on their 50th wedding anniversary by throwing a reaffirmation party. Their eldest son, Len, delivered these remarks:

LEN:

Mom, Dad, we, your children, have always looked to you for a model of true love. We know that you've had some hard times—most of them probably due to us. But as Ghandi said, *Unity, to be real, must stand the severest strain without breaking.* (HARDSHIP) And we can see that your unity is real.

We found this poem excerpt from Ralph Waldo Emerson, and it reminded all of us of what we've learned about love from watching you two:

Give all in love;
Obey thy heart;
Friends, kindred, days,
Estate, good fame,
Plans, credit, and the Muse,
Nothing refuse.
(SHARING THE WEALTH)

We want to thank you for all that you have taught us, tell you how proud we are of you and your ability to stay so obviously in love all these years and let you know that we hope to marry as well as you did.

∽

Gina and Mark work as a writing team. In the ten years of their marriage, they have gone from struggling poets to highly successful scriptwriters. They have many friends whose marriages have not been able to weather similar changes. Throughout their marriage, they've always talked through everything, and wanted a vow renewal service to acknowledge the importance of communication in their relationship

and to show how much their love has stayed the same, even though their circumstances have changed.

MARK:

Thank you all for coming to our reaffirmation ceremony. It's indulgent of us, we fear, to ask you to dress up in fancy clothes and drive up here for yet another wedding ceremony—so soon on the heels of the last. But Gina and I feel so fortunate to have had you all in our lives during these past ten tumultuous, wonderful years, and we wanted to share our reaffirmation with you. And, the food, I am assured, is going to be great.

Gina and I credit our continued happiness to our ability to discuss anything with each other, in the most minute detail, sometimes to the chagrin of everyone else in the room. As the author Cyril Connolly said, *Marriage is the permanent conversation between two people who talk over everything and everyone until death breaks the record.* (FOREVER LOVE)

Certainly we've talked over everything and everyone. Don't worry, anything we've said about any of you has been totally positive, of course. I am truly grateful for having someone with whom I can communicate so well.

And I am eternally grateful for Gina in other ways, too. I know I would not be standing here today, on my lawn, in front of this house, if it weren't for her. There's a synergy in marriage that I have never known before in my life. As the philosopher Nietzsche said, *Marriage: that I call the will of two to create the one who is more than those who created it.* (SOUL MATES/SYNERGY)

Whatever we've created together is more than I could have dreamed of doing alone.

Finally, I want to say, that while much has been made of our external success, ultimately, money is irrelevant. To quote one more great philosopher, Elvis Presley: *Give me a cave up in the mountains or a shack down by the sea,*

And I will be in heaven, honey, if you are there with me. (VALUES)

GINA:

My sentiments exactly. There's one more thing I'd like to add though. The success of our marriage—for me—has been in large part due to Mark's unerring ability to help me become the person I wanted to be. To put it in a nut-shell:

I love you, not for what you are, but for what
I am when I am with you. I love you, not
only for what you have made of yourself, but
for what you are making of me. I love you
for the part of me that you bring out; I love
you for putting your hand into my heaped-up
heart and passing over all the foolish, weak
things that you can't help dimly seeing there,
and for drawing out into the lights all the
beautiful belongings that no one else had
looked quite far enough to find. I love you
because you are helping me to make of the
lumber of my life not a tavern but a temple;
out of the works of my every day, not a
reproach, but a song. I love you because
you have done more than any creed could
have done to make me good, and more
than any fate could have done to make
me happy. You have done it without
a touch, without a word, without a sign.
You have done it by being yourself.
perhaps that is what being in love
means, after all
(ROY CROFT, GROWTH)

I want to thank Mark for helping provide the meaning in my life, and to thank all of you for supporting this marriage.

REAFFIRMATION RECEPTION

Your reaffirmation reception can be any type of party you want. You may want something more relaxed than your first wedding, or one that includes many of the traditional wedding reception elements such as a receiving line, toasts and cake cutting. Turn to Chapter 8 for suggestions for personalizing your reception.

～ Reaffirmation Extras ～

Rings That Sing

Get your old rings engraved with a line from your favorite poem, or get new gold rings made inscribed with this fragment from Katherine Lee Bates: *Old love is gold love.* (IT'S BETTER WHEN YOU'RE OLDER)

You also may want to give each other a locket or other piece of jewelry with a special phrase inscribed, such as this fragment from Theodore Parker: *A happy wedlock is a long falling in love.* (IT'S BETTER WHEN YOU'RE OLDER) Or give a long necklace made of three intertwined chains, hung with a pendant with these words by Robert Burton: *No cord nor cable can so forcibly draw, or hold so fast, as love can do with a twined thread.* (LOVE)

Words for Children

Include your children by giving them a book of poems by your favorite poet or a collection of poems you've culled from this book that encompass your thoughts about marriage that you want to hand down.

Your Original Guest Book

Let guests pore over the words they wrote long ago. Have a new book for them to write in now.

Wedding Favors

Give guests favors that say it best—a book of poems or a CD with your favorite song. If it's a family-only affair, give a family portrait in a silver frame engraved with this quote fragment: *Family love is . . . this shared belonging to a chain of generations.* (MICHAEL IGNATIEFF, FAMILY)

Or give a scroll with your favorite poem, or a book of "quotes through the years"—something you create yourself with quotes that sum up each stage of your life. Turn to Chapter 6 and Chapter 8 for other favor ideas.

Chapter 10

Extra Touches

Now that you've got the basics covered, there are loads of other ways to include creative language throughout your wedding—from invitations to thank-you notes. Here are some suggestions:

∾ Send Inspired Invitations ∾

Why stick to the traditional "We request the honor of your presence . . ." invitation when you can make your wedding stand out from the moment you announce it? Include a line from your favorite song or a short selection of poetry at the top or bottom of your wedding invitation. If you're having a small wedding, or one with a *big* budget, send a single-song CD with your favorite romantic song along with the wedding invite.

Sample Invitations

**Now join your hands,
and with your hands your hearts.***

Mr. and Mrs. Chuck Nelson
Request the honor of your presence
At the marriage of their daughter

Sandra Nelson
To
Michael Garber
Saturday, the Sixth of June
At 2 o'clock
The Renaissance Center
Detroit, MI

Jean and Jo, both in their mid-40s, have been married before. This is the second wedding for both of them and they are hosting the wedding themselves, with the help of their children.

Amy and Sandy Shenkar
and
Brian and David King

---

*(WILLIAM SHAKESPEARE, *KING HENRY VI*/WEDDING DAY)

Request the honor of your presence at the marriage of their parents
Jean Shenkar
and
Jo King

Saturday, May 22
At 11 o'clock
Golden Gate Park
San Francisco, CA

True love . . . is always young in the heart

❧ Launch a Wedding Web Site ❧

Set up a wedding Web site to keep all your guests informed about the pending event. Include your favorite music on your site and a few quotes throughout. Ask guests to send in their favorite quotes and create a quote library that guests can click on.

❧ Give Gift Baskets for ❧ Out-of-Town Guests

Make welcoming gift baskets and put them in the hotel rooms of out-of-town guests. Include a local map, a list of current events, attractions and phone numbers and something edible made in your hometown. Tie up the basket with a ribbon you've had printed with these lines: *Remember*

---

*(HONORÉ DE BALZAC, LOVE KEEPS YOU YOUNG)

this . . . that very little is needed to make a happy life. (HAPPINESS, JOY, AND LAUGH-TER) Thank you for coming to our wedding!" Look through the front of this book for other welcoming words.

You also can handwrite your quote with a silver or gold pen on the ribbon, tissue paper or welcome card.

Present Each Other with
Personal Presents

Traditionally, the bride and groom give each other wedding gifts as well. Make yours meaningful by giving a piece of your mind, too. Present your soon-to-be with a silver ring, engraved with these words by Geoffrey Chaucer: *Go little ring to that same sweet that hath my heart in her domain . . .* (CONVICTION/DEVOTION) Or give your stargazing sweetheart a telescope, and include a card inspired by Blanch Shoemaker Wagstaff: *You are the evening star at the end of day.* (CONVICTION/DEVOTION)

Send Nontraditional Thank-Yous

When ordering your invitations, don't forget to order thank-you notes, too. Have your thank-you notes printed with your favorite quote or quip, for example, this phrase from Thomas à Kempis: *A wise lover values not so much the gift of the lover as the love of the giver.* (VALUES)

Throw Verbal Confetti

Instead of throwing rice or birdseed, have your guests toss confetti quotes—little strips of paper with wedding words printed on them. You can make your confetti on a computer and print it out on colored paper. Appoint a few relatives or friends to "confetti duty" and have them pass out packets of confetti to throw as you leave the ceremony. Your confetti might include these lines: *For thy sweet love remember'd such wealth brings/That then I scorn to change my state with kings.* (SHAKESPEARE, VALUES); *Let all the joys be as the month of May/And all thy days be as a marriage day.* (FRANCIS QUARLES, WEDDING DAY); and *The supreme sight on the black earth . . . is the one you love* (SAPPHO, CONVICTION/DEVOTION). Look through the front of this book for other ideas, paying particular attention to the "Love," "Passion," "Soul Mates/Synergy," and "Values" sections.

∾ Decorate the Getaway Car ∾

Why stick to JUST MARRIED when there is an entire rear window on which to write your thoughts? Your friends might write, *I am prepared for this voyage, and for anything else you may care to mention.* (JOHN ASHBERRY, MARRIAGE ITSELF).

After Words

Once the wedding is over, the presents are opened, the thank-you notes written, the work is done, right? Wrong.

Now is when the real work begins. And the real fun. Your wedding, despite all the time and effort and expense, is just a one-day event. It isn't, ultimately, the part that matters most. What matters most is the marriage. You might spend a year planning the perfect wedding, but if you let your efforts toward each other end there, your marriage would be nothing compared to that one day. Yes, your wedding should be everything you dream, but it should not be the best day of your life. It should be the beginning of the best *days* of your life.

You can use the quotes in this book to continue to nurture your relationship. Refer to them periodically to help you express how you feel. Write your favorite quote on a card and prop it up against the orange juice glass in the morning. Include your favorite line on an anniversary note. When expressing thanks for something—a gift or an uncommon consideration—write it down, and add a quote from this book. There are hundreds of ways to say, "I love you." The important thing is to say it, and to keep making it true.

But don't stop there. A happy marriage, ultimately, is not just about falling in love and living happily ever after—sitting on the couch with your new spouse, eating Chinese food and watching TV. A good marriage produces a strength and an energy that is more than the sum of the two of you. Take that energy and spread it outward, toward the world. Share your passion with others. Use it to help make the world around you a more loving place. To pull a quote from this book:

> *Any marriage which is turned in upon itself, in which the bride and groom simply gaze obsessively at one another, goes out after a time.*
>
> *A marriage which really works is one which works for others. Marriage has both a private face and a public importance . . . Those who are married live happily ever after the wedding day if they persevere in the real adventure, which is the royal task of creating each other and creating a more loving world.*
>
> –Archbishop of Canterbury, on the marriage of Queen Elizabeth II*

---

*(MARRIAGE ITSELF)

Bibliography

Anastasio, Janet, and Bevilacqua, Michelle. *The Everything Wedding Vows Book.* Adams Media Corporation, Holbrook, MA. 1994.

Argy, Josy, and Riches, Wendy. *Britain's Royal Brides.* David & Charles: Newton Abbot. 1975.

Bailey, Beth L. *From Front Porch to Back Seat: Courtship in Twentieth-Century America.* Johns Hopkins University Press: Baltimore, MD. 1988.

Balliett, Will, ed. *The Little Book of Weddings: An Anthology.* Atlantic Monthly Press: NY. 1996.

Bernard, Jessie Shirley. *Dating, Mating and Marriage: A Documentary-Case Approach.* H. Allen: Cleveland. 1958.

Brill, Mordecai L. *Write Your Own Wedding.* New Century: Piscataway, NJ. 1985.

Burgess, Ernest Watson, and Wallin, Paul. *Engagement and Marriage.* Lippincott: Philadelphia, PA. 1953.

Butler, Becky, ed. *Ceremonies of the Heart: Celebrating Lesbian Unions.* Seal Press: Seattle, WA. 1990.

Butterick Publishing Company. *Weddings and Wedding Anniversaries.* The Butterick Publishing Co.: NY. 1905.

Caldwell, Louis O. *Through the Years: An Anniversary Remembrance.* Abingdon Press: Nashville, TN. 1975.

Canfield, J. Douglas. *Word As Bond in English Literature from the Middle Ages to the Restoration.* University of Pennsylvania Press, Philadelphia, PA. 1989.

Cartland, Barbara. *Etiquette for Love and Romance.* Pocket Books: NY. 1984.

Cole, Emma Aubert. *The Modern Bride Book of Etiquette and Entertaining.* Ziff-Davis Publishing Company: NY. 1961.

Cole, Harriette. *Jumping the Broom Wedding Workbook: A Step-by-Step Write-in Guide to Planning the Perfect African-American Wedding.* Henry Holt: NY. 1996.

Cook, Ann Jennalie. *Making a Match: Courtship in Shakespeare and His Society.* Princeton University Press: Princeton, NJ. 1991.

Davenport, Gwen. *Great Loves in Legend and Life.* Franklin Watts: NY. 1964.

Davis, Randall, ed. *Advice to Young Ladies: from "The London Journal" of 1855 and 1862.* Methuen: London. 1933.

Eisen, Armand. *The Wedding Book: A Bride's Memento.* Ariel Books, Andrews and McMeel: Kansas City, MO. 1985.

Eisen, Armand. *Marriage: Altered States.* Ariel Books, Andrew and McMeel: Kansas City, MO. 1992.

Gillis, John R. *For Better, for Worse: British Marriages, 1600 to the Present.* Oxford University Press: NY. 1988.

Hart, Cynthia, and Grossman, John. *Forget-Me-Nots: A Victorian Book of Love.* Workman Publishers: NY. 1990.

Hass, Robert, and Mitchell, Stephen, eds. *Into the Garden: A Wedding Anthology: Poetry and Prose on Love and Marriage.* HarperCollins: NY. 1993.

Hefter, Wendy Chernak. *The Complete Jewish Wedding Planner.* Harper & Row: San Francisco, CA. 1998.

Holliday, Carl. *Wedding Customs Then and Now.* Stratford Company: Boston, MA. 1919.

Ishee, Mark. *Wedding Toasts and Traditions.* JM Productions: Brentwood, TN. 1986.

Jeffrey, Barbara. *Wedding Speeches and Toasts.* Slough (Bucks.): New York. 1966.

Kingma, Daphne Rose. *Weddings from the Heart: Contemporary and Traditional Ceremonies for an Unforgettable Wedding.* Conari Press: Berkeley, CA. 1995.

Klausner, Abraham J. *Weddings: A Complete Guide to All Religious and Interfaith Marriage Services.* Alpha Publishing Company: Columbus, OH. 1986.

Lalli, Cele Goldsmith. *Modern Bride Wedding Celebrations: The Complete Wedding Planner for Today's Bride.* J. Wiley & Sons: NY. 1992.

Lansky, Bruce, ed. *For Better and for Worse.* Meadowbrook Press: Minnetonka, MN. 1997.

Lockwood, Georgene Muller. *Your Victorian Wedding: A Modern Guide for the Romantic Bride.* Prentice Hall: NY. 1992.

Loeb, Evelyn (compiled by). *Love Poems and Love Letters.* Peter Pauper Press: White Plains: NY. 1994.

Lystra, Karen. *Searching the Heart: Women, Men, and Romantic Love in Nineteenth-Century America.* Oxford University Press: NY. 1989.

Mayo, Simon. *The Big Match: The Art of Getting and Staying Married—In Several Hundred Easy Steps.* Marshall Pickering: London. 1993.

McGuire, Kim. *The Irish Wedding Book.* Wolfhound Press: Dublin. 1994.

McWilliams, Peter. *I Marry You Because . . .* Wilshire Publications: Carpinteria, CA. 1997.

Moore, June Langley-Levy. *The Bride's Book or, Young Housewife's Compendium.* Gerald Howe: London. 1932.

Nelson, Gertrud Mueller, and Witt, Christopher. *Sacred Threshold, Rituals and Readings for a Wedding Spirit.* Image Books (published by Doubleday): NY. 1998.

Newman, Paul S., ed. *Happy Anniversary.* C. R. Gibson Company: Norwalk, CN. 1975.

Post, Elizabeth L. *Emily Post's Complete Book of Wedding Etiquette.* Harper & Row: NY. 1982.

Rothman, Ellen K. *Hands and Hearts: A History of Courtship in America.* Basic Books: NY. 1984.

St. Marie, Satenig S., and Flaherty, Carolyn. *Romantic Victorian Weddings, Then & Now.* Dutton Studio Books: NY. 1992.

Sanger, Margaret. *Happiness in Marriage.* Maxwell Reprint Company: Elmsford, NY. 1995.

Scheu-Riesz, Helene, ed. *Will You Marry Me? Proposal Letters of Seven Centuries.* Island Workshop Press Co-op: NY. 1940.

Signature Bride Magazine, eds. *Going to the Chapel: From Traditional to African-Inspired, and Everything in Between—The Ultimate Wedding Guide for Today's Black Couple.* G. P. Putnam's Sons: NY. 1998.

Smith, Marie D., and Durbin, Louise. *White House Brides.* Acropolis Books: Washington, D.C. 1996.

Spender, Dale. *Weddings and Wives.* Penguin Books: NY. 1994.

Stuart, Paul. *Conditioned Love: The Art of Winning and Holding a Man's Love.* Franklin & Freeman Publishing Company: Philadelphia, PA. 1952.

Thomas, Pamela. *Bridal Guide: A Complete Guide to Weddings in Churches and Synagogues.* Fifth Avenue Brides Publishing Company: La Crosse, WI. 1987.

Tober, Barbara. *The Bride: A Celebration.* H. N. Abrams Company: NY. 1984.

Turner, E. S. *A History of Courting.* M. Joseph: London. 1954.

Warner, Gary. *Love, Honor and Cherish: The Greatest Wedding Moments from All My Children, General Hospital, and One Life to Live.* Hyperion: NY. 1998.

Weaver, Joanna. *With This Ring.* Waterbrook Press: Colorado Springs, CO. 1999.

Welker, Roy Anson. *Courtship and Marriage: A Guide to Study.* L.D.S. Department of Education: Salt Lake City, UT. 1940.

Wilson, Barbara. *The Bride's School: Complete Book of Engagement and Wedding Etiquette.* Hawthorn Books: NY. 1959.

Zimmerman, Catherine S. *The Bride's Book: A Pictorial History of American Bridal Dress.* Arbor House: NY. 1985.
————. *How Heroes of Fiction Propose and How Heroines Reply: Together with Familiar Quotations in Poetry and Prose: With Parallel Passages from the Most Famous Writers of the World.* P. F. Collier: NY. 1890.

People

Ackerman, Diane

Adams, John

Adams, John Quincy

Addison, Joseph

Adler, Mortimer

Affleck, Ben

Akhmatova, Anna

Akhtar, Hoshang N.

Alcott, Louisa May

Aleichem, Shalom

Allen, Gracie

Allen, Woody

Amichai, Yehuda

Anderson, Maxwell

Anspacher, L. K.

Arberry, A. J.

Archbishop of Canterbury

Archduchess Maria Louise of Austria

Archilochos

Arnold, Edwin

Ashberry, John

Auden, W. H.

Austen, Jane

Bacall, Lauren

Bacon, Francis

Badran, Margo

Baldwin, Alec

Baldwin, James

Balzac, Honoré de

Bardot, Brigitte

Barrie, Sir James

Barry, Dave

Barry, Lynda

Barrymore, Drew

Basinger, Kim

Bates, Katherine Lee

Batten, Susan

Beaumont, Madame LePrince de

Beecher, Henry Ward

Behan, Brandan

Bennett, Joan

Bennett, William Cox

Bergman, Ingrid
Bernard, Jessie
Berry, Wendell
Berry, William
Beuchner, Frederick
Bickerstaffe, Isaac
Bierce, Ambrose
Billings, Josh
Bismarck, Otto von
Blucher, Field Marshal Gebhard
    Leberecht
Blumenthal, Michael
Bly, Robert
Bogart, Humphrey
Boleyn, Anne
Bonhoeffer, Dietrich
Bono, Sonny
Borge, Victor
Boswell, James
Bower, David
Bradstreet, Anne
Brandeis, Louis
Brawne, Fanny
Brickner, B. R.
Bricusse, Leslie
Brontë, Emily
Browning, Elizabeth Barrett
Browning, Robert
Bruckner, Anton
Bryson, Peabo
Burgess, Anthony
Burns, Robert
Burton, Robert

Bush, Barbara
Butler, Samuel
Cage, Nicolas
Cain, Dean
Caldwell, Louis O.
Campbell, Joseph
Campbell, Mrs. Patrick
Carey, Philip
Carlyle, Thomas
Carpenter, Charlotte
Carroll, Jonathan
Carter, Marcia
Cartwright, William
Chaucer, Geoffrey
Cheever, John
Chennault, Anna
Cheraker, Albert
Chesnutt, Mark
Chesterton, G. K.
Christie, Agatha
Chung, Ling
Churchill, Winston
Cicero
Clooney, Rosemary
Cohn, Marc
Collette, Toni
Collyer, Robert
Colton, Charles Caleb
Confucius
Congreve, William
Connolly, Cyril
Conrad, J.
Cotton, Nathan

Court, Diane
Cowper, William
Craik, Dinah Maria Mulock
Crane, Frank
Crawford, Joan
Crawley, Ernest
Creeley, Robert
Croft, Ray
Cromwell, Oliver
Cronkite, Betsy
Crowel, Marnie Reed
Crystal, Billy
cummings, e. e.
Cusack, John
Dacier, Anne
Daley, Cass
Dante
Darden, Christopher
David, Alfred
David, Mary Elizabeth
Davis, Flora
Davis, Hal
Davis, Nina
Dayton, Dorothy
De Vries, Peter
DeLange, Eddie
Delgado, Maggie
Dell'oso, Anna Maria
DePaiva, James
Diaz, Cameron
DiCaprio, Leonardo
Dickens, Charles
Dickinson, Emily

Dimock, Edward C., Jr.
DiPaolo, Dante
Disraeli, Benjamin
Dix, Dorothy
Dobler, Lloyd
Dodds, Robert C.
Donne, John
Dostoevsky, Fyodor
Dozier, Lamont
Draper, Eliza
Dugan, Alan
Dunn, Stephen
Dunne, Finley Peter
Durant, Will
Dyke, Henry van
Ebb, Fred
Edgeworth, Maria
Edward VIII
Coleridge, Samuel Taylor
Edwards, Amelia B.
Einstein, Albert
Eisenhower, Dwight D.
Ekland, Britt
Eliot, George
Emerson, Ralph Waldo
Emperor Napoleon
Enslin, Ted
Erasmus
Errico, Melissa
Fielding, Henry
Fiennes, Joseph
Fisher, George
Fitzgerald, F. Scott

Flaubert, Gustave
Flood, Corey
Fonda, Jane
Fonda, Peter
Ford, John
Forster, E. M.
Fosdick, Harry Emerson
Fox, Vivian A.
Franken, Rose
Franklin, Benjamin
Frederick, Augustus
Freud, Sigmund
Friedan, Betty
Fromm, Erich
Frost, Robert
Fuller, Thomas
Gabor, Zsa Zsa
Gairdner, Temple
Gammie, Susan
Gandhi, Mahatma
Gautier, Theophile
Gay, John
Gibran, Kahlil
Gilbert, Sir William
Gilbert, W. S.
Giles, W.
Gilman, Caroline
Giovanni, Nikki
Gist, Nathan H.
Gladstone, William
Goethe, Johann Wolfgang von
Goldsmith, Oliver
Goldwyn, Samuel

Golightly, Holly
Goodman, Roy
Gordon, George, Lord Byron
Gordy, Berry
Grable, Betty
Grant, Hugh
Grant, Lee
Gray, Thomas
Greene, Graham
Greer, Germaine
Grossman, John
Guest, Edgar
Guitry, Sacha
Halevi, Judah
Halifax, Lord
Hammarskjöld, Dag
Hanks, Tom
Harburg, E. Y.
Hardy, Thomas
Hart, Cynthia
Hart, Lorenz
Harvest, Christopher
Haskell, Susan
Hawthorne, Nathaniel
Hayes, Helen
Hazlitt, William
Heine, Heinrich
Hellman, Lillian
Henry, O.
Hepburn, Audrey
Hepburn, Katharine
Herbert, George
Herold, Don

Lewis, Michael
Li Tai Po
Lincoln, Abraham
Lindbergh, Anne Morrow
Lindbergh, Charles
Loewe, Frederick
Longfellow, Henry Wadsworth
Lord, Tracey
Love, Adelaide
Lover, Samuel
Lovett, Lyle
Lowell, Amy
Lowenthal, Marvin
Lulham, Hubberton
Lupus, Marlin Finch
Luther, Martin
Lynne, Gloria
Lyttleton, Lord
Mace, David R.
Machado, Antonio
Mackenzie, Charlie
MacLaine, Shirley
Malet, L.
Marcil, Vanessa
Margulies, Juliana
Marryatt, Florence
Marshall, Peter
Marx, Harpo
Matthews, Denise
Maugham, W. Somerset
Maule, Brad
Mauriac, François
Maurois, André

Mayo, Simon
McCant, Jerry
McClain, Cady
McConaughey, Matthew
McCready, Mindy
McCullers, Carson
McEnroe, Patrick
McIntosh, Millicent Carey
McLaughlin, Mignon
McWilliams, Peter
Melville, Herman
Menander
Mencken, H. L.
Mendoza, Antonio Hurtado de
Menninger, Dr. Karl
Meredith, George
Meredith, William
Michaels, Harriet
Milligan, Spike
Milton, John
Mistral, Gabriella
Mitchell, Langdon
Mitchell, Stephen
Montaigne, Michel de
Moon, Reverend Sun Myung
Moore, Thomas
Moreau, Jeanne
Mother Teresa
Mozart, Wolfgang Amadeus
Mueller, Lisel
Munch-Bellinghausen, Josef von
Murdoch, Iris
Murray, D. Christie

Spender, Lynne

Spenser, Edmund

Spinoza, Baruch

Spock, Benjamin

Sprat, Thomas

Stael, Mme. de

Stamos, John

Stanley, A. P.

Steele, Richard

Stein, Gertrude

Steinem, Gloria

Sterne, Laurence

Stevenson, Adlai

Stevenson, Robert Louis

Steward, James

Stoddard, Sarah

Strindberg, August

Styne, Jule

Suard, Jean

Sullivan, Sir Arthur

Summerskill, Baroness Edith

Sunday, Billy

Swift, Jonathan

Swinburne, Algernon Charles

Tao-Sheng, Kuan

Tarbuck, Barbara

Tarkington, Booth

Taylor, Jeremy

Taylor, Lili

Teasdale, Sara

Teilhard de Chardin, Pierre

Tennyson, Lord Alfred

Thackery, Maria

Thackery, W. M.

Thatcher, David

Thatcher, Margaret

Thayer, Ethel

Thayer, Norman

Thomas, Joe

Thompson, Sophie

Thomson, James

Thoreau, Henry David

Thurber, James

Tibullus

Tillich, Paul

Timmins, Michael

Tolstoy, Leo

Tournier, Paul

Tov, Baal Shem

Townsend, Mary Ashley

Tracy, Spencer

Trampedach, Mathilde

Travis, Nancy

Trollope, Anthony

Truman, Harry S.

Tu Fu

Tzu, Lao

Uhl, Frieda

Ustinov, Peter

Valéry, Paul

Van Heusen, James

Vanderbilt, Amy

Vanderbilt, Gloria

Varjack, Paul

Vidypati

Viorst, Judith

Voltaire
Wagstaff, Blanch Shoemaker
Waldrop, Mark
Walker, James J.
Walker, Tonja
Warren, Diane
Washington, George
Weaver, Joanna
West, Bob
West, Mae
Whitehead, Gillian
Whitley, Keith
Whitman, Keith
Whitman, Walt
Widow Gibbs
Wilde, Oscar
Wildhorn, Frank

Williamson, Marianne
Willis, N. P.
Winslet, Kate
Winston, Liz
Wolkstein, Diane
Wonder, Stevie
Wood, Ira
Wood, Katherine
Wood, Leland Foster
Woodward, Joanne
Woolsey, John M.
Wordsworth, William
Wroe, Martin
Yeats, William Butler
Yeston
Zeman, Jacklyn

Permission Credits

cerpts from *People* magazine, July 1995 and June 1998 editions. Reprinted by permission of *People* magazine. Copyright © 1995, 1998 Time Inc. All rights reserved.

Excerpt from "Gift from the Sea," by Anne Morrow Lindbergh, reprinted by permission of Pantheon Books, a division of Random House, Inc.

Excerpt from, "The Chuppah," from *My Mother's Body,* by Marge Piercy. Copyright © 1985 by Marge Piercy, reprinted by permission of Alfred A. Knopf, a division of Random House, Inc.

Excerpt from *Harem Years: The Memoirs of an Egyptian Feminist* by Huda Shaarawi translated and with an introduction by Margot Badran. Translation copyright © 1986 by Margot Badran. Reprinted by permission of The Feminist Press at The City University of New York.

Excerpt from "as the sea is marvelous," form "Amores," by e. e. cummings copyright © 1923, 1951, © 1991 by the Trustees for the e. e. cummings Trust. Copyright © 1976 by George James Firmage, from *Complete Poems: 1904–1962* by e. e. cummings, edited by George J. Firmage. Used by permission of Liveright Publishing Corporation.

About the Authors

Wendy Paris is a freelance writer living in New York City. She has written about weddings, marriage and honeymoons for *Bride's Magazine, Modern Bride,* and *The Knot,* and about other topics for *Self, Glamour, Family Circle, More, Condé Nast Traveler,* www.gymamerica.com and www.working-woman.com. She has also worked as a television producer and reporter and contributes essays to several National Public Radio shows.

Andrew Chesler is coauthor of *Criminal Quotes: The 1001 Most Bizarre Things Ever Said by History's Outlaws, Gangsters, Despots and Other Evil-Doers* (Visible Ink Press, 1997) and *The Encyclopedia of American Family Names* (HarperCollins, 1995). He works as an artist, lives in New York City and exhibits there and abroad.